CHURCH BUILDING

IS VOLUME

120

OF THE

Twentieth Century Encyclopedia of Catholicism

UNDER SECTION

XII

CATHOLICISM AND THE ARTS

IT IS ALSO THE

136TH

VOLUME IN ORDER OF PUBLICATION

THE TWENTIETH CENTURY ENCYCLOPEDIA OF CATHOLICISM

Edited by HENRI DANIEL-ROPS of the Académie Française

CHURCH BUILDING

By JOSEPH RYKWERT

HAWTHORN BOOKS · PUBLISHERS · New York

First Edition, January, 1966

NIHIL OBSTAT

Lionel Swain, S.T.L., L.S.S.

   Censor Deputatus

IMPRIMATUR

✠ Patritius Casey

   Vicarius Generalis

Westmonasterii, die XXVII NOVEMBRIS MCMLXV

9549

CONTENTS

INTRODUCTION

The idea that every building is a kind of machine which must be workable and efficient has become very familiar, though many people might think, with reason, that this idea cannot apply to churches. The elaborate and varied forms of church building seem quite often to arise in answer to arbitrary and irrational demands. And yet when looked at closer these demands fall into a pattern, and the pattern is legible.

"Church" is a word which has a number of meanings and the church building must do a number of different things. The church is firstly the community of all believers; and inevitably, therefore, a collectivity. The most obvious thing the church has to do is to keep the weather out so that this group can worship their Maker in all seasons. This worship is a public act which makes the group into a community. By this act the collectivity turns to God, but also through this act a new meaning is given to the human relations between its members.

Beyond keeping the weather out the building which shelters the community must carry out tasks related to both human and divine functions, tasks which are more complex and more interesting than that of keeping out the weather. Some of these tasks may, at first sight, appear contradictory. So the church must be a temple, because it is a place where the Christians witness and perform a sacrifice, the sacrifice of Calvary; secondly, it must be a dining hall centred on a table because the liturgy is a meal shared by the Christian community. Again, as the Christian community considers itself the mystical body of Christ, so the church building in which it is gathered must give countenance to this belief: must in some way represent a complete human being. At the same time the Christian sees himself as travelling through the world in a ship, captained by St Peter, as Noah travelled over the flood in his ark. This again should be demonstrated by some association established in the church building.

All this does not mean, of course, that the church should *look like* a man or a ship, but that its form should be of such a kind that these images can be associated in some way with the building.

The first group of functions which I suggested, that of the temple, the dining hall, are concerned with what goes on inside the building, the other two, the church as a body and a ship, are concerned with the actual shape of the building itself. You may see that while the first group of functions is symbolic, the second is metaphoric. There are several other metaphors which a church building may suggest. You may consider it as a cave in which Mother Church shelters her children; or as a palace where the King of Glory holds his court on earth; or as a gate through which we must pass to gain salvation. There are many other ways, depending on the way Christians are thinking at the time when the church is built, or of the particular situation of the church building itself: whether it is a pilgrimage chapel or a great cathedral, as to how these metaphorical associations are suggested in the building.

The first building of the Christian Church was the upper room in which our Lord and his disciples kept the Passover, but it was not until the group of first Christians was welded into a powerful unity at Pentecost that the meaning of that first eucharistic meal became evident and the Church set out on her history. These first Christians did not at once set about building. They gathered at first in buildings which already existed, almost exclusively in private houses, later also in public buildings though hardly ever in buildings destined for pagan worship.

There were times and places, particularly in these first days, when Christian worship was forbidden by law and the Eucharist celebrated in hiding. Inevitably when Christian churches came to be built they retained some vestiges of those buildings in which their worship took form. As with the church building, so with the outward forms of worship: Christians used the ceremonies and trappings current in the world to dignify ceremonies and functions instituted by the Church for her own purposes. The politeness and courtesy of the Eucharist will always use the forms of politeness current in the place where the liturgy developed: they will rarely be the forms of religious worship since the forms of pagan religions would not be apposite to the needs of the Christian community at prayer, but they will always make use of the commonplaces of polite ceremonious behaviour which exists in all societies.

So one source of the Latin liturgy was the formal proceedings of the Roman law courts (as opposed to Roman religious practice) while the liturgy of the Greek and Slavonic Churches has more in common with the extravagantly elaborate proceedings of the Hellenistic royal palace than with the sober transactions of a court of law. But the transition between a meal taken in common and the fully formalized liturgy with which we are familiar took many centuries, and the long line of development, a line which will not end until the Church has stopped growing—that is, until the end of the world—has shaped and transformed the actual structure of church building: liturgy is the living movement around which a church building is a shell or a shelter and so it is inevitably shaped and moulded by the movement of the liturgy. Though buildings, being solid things which sometimes take centuries to complete, always lag one or two steps behind the changes of thought and devotion of the Christian community, nevertheless they could be thought of as a reflection of these changes, and to consider them in terms of such changes will be a much more useful approach to understanding them, than to run simply through a catalogue of styles which the usual handbook offers.

In the liturgy in the prayer which commemorates our Lord's actions on earth the Church remembers particularly the passion, resurrection and the ascension. Each of these is recollected not only in the words of the celebrant but in some physical feature of the church; inanimate physical features which act in harmony with the movements of the living worshippers: so that the altar itself which is often shaped like a sarcophagus (and whose function is underlined by the five crosses marked on the altar slab to commemorate the five wounds of Christ) is the memorial of the passion and death; the eucharistic elements, as well as the celebrant who offers them, are the risen Lord; the ascension is remembered usually in a picture which appears in most churches, certainly throughout the first thousand years of Christian art, of our Lord in glory. The picture appears at some climactic point in the church building, over the altar or over the triumphal arch—or even looking down from the central dome. This sequence of references relates to the way in which the church building was a representation of the whole universe as it is understood by theology. This representation varied according to place, theological developments and building technique. To take one instance, however, in the Latin basilica, the body of the church, the nave, represented this world in which we live; the chancel arch, death and judgement through which we must pass as through a triumphal arch to attain the chancel, heaven.

The church building not only commemorates the great moments of our Lord's life but also the places in which these events took place: in the church building real time, the time we experience and the time about which historians write, is brought into touch with the short span of time through which the salvation of humankind was operated. From the Christian point of view this short span shares the characteristics of time as we know it with those of eternity, since it is the time during which God, as it were pierced time and made it touch eternity. So the church building which carries within it the summing up of that short period, not only commemorates the events of our Lord's life but in the act of commemoration actually re-enacts all the Gospel scenes which took place in those days around Jerusalem. In some way, therefore, the church must not just represent but, through the eucharistic action, be identical with the upper room of the Last Supper as well as the two mountains of the anamnesis: Calvary and Olivet.

The liturgy is cast into the outward forms of the period in which it was formulated, but it must also recall forms in which Israel, the people of God, worshipped before the coming of our Lord: it must recall the scriptural types to which he referred himself, Abel, Abraham and Melchisedech. That is why the altar of the church, which, as I said earlier, is in one sense Christ himself, represents also the table round which the Last Supper was taken in the upper room; and must also contain the idea of the altar at which sacrifices were offered at the Temple in Jerusalem: and so include in itself all those other altars in scripture referring ultimately to that first one on which Abel offered his lamb.

For the very simple forms, which I have so far described, to carry such a rich amalgam of different ideas the church building must be brought to life with all its complex overtones when it is filled by the public prayer of worshipping Christians. In the past the church was never designed as a place of retirement for private prayer; it was always considered primarily as a hall for the public worship of the Christian community: principally as this worship is expressed in the eucharistic liturgy—though other sacramental forms of public worship were always considered. But if it is the body of worshippers which gives life to the building, the cold forms must also have the power to speak to the worshipper. The message which the church building carries must therefore be comprehensible to the worshipper if it is to be of any value; and not only to the worshipper but also, if possible, to the ordinary passer-by. The forms of discourse, therefore, the visual language used by the architect and the artists who conceive and decorate the building, must be easily understood. They will speak, in the first place, to their contemporaries for whom they are working directly. Since there is no such thing as a timeless language, since language moves and changes with the passing of time, the designer must make use of the same visual terms, the same images, as the people whom he is directly addressing. When he and they are dead the building and its message will become the heritage of future generations and their discourse of that moment (whenever it may have been) will pass into the common language of all worshippers. This message will therefore resist the corrupting influence of time only if it is urgent enough to seize on the imagination of the designer's contemporaries so that it becomes a standard to which they can refer their total visual experience.

The earliest churches were planted in a pagan world and offered a spiritual home to people with a most diverse background; Jews, Samaritans, devotees of the various mystic cults and pagans from all parts of the world, drew on prototypes which related to the previous experience of all those different early Christians. This does not mean that the Christian religion was unduly eclectic or that the art which it inspired was entirely derivative. On the contrary, I would like to emphasize that the artists of the early Church were inspired by the pastoral need to which their art was an answer, a need to address their contemporaries in a visual language whose vocabulary made sense in terms of the whole environment in which the early Christian lived. The desire to see absolute originality in early Christian art springs from a misunderstanding about the function of art in the Church, which is dual: to create a harmonious and edifying environment for Christian worship and to speak to the worshippers—in visual terms—about the foundations of their faith.

The artists of the early Church, therefore, would have done the Christian community a disservice had they been concerned to create a completely new visual language. Their task was to transmute the existing forms of visual, plastic discourse and charge them with a new meaning. The form of a building, moreover, is not arbitrary but grows within the pattern of use, it is shaped by the movement people make inside it. The Church, therefore, took over certain architectural forms from the pagan world and used them to enclose analogous functions in the pattern of movement made by Christian worship; and so gave them a new and extended meaning.

The liturgy owed a debt to the procedure of Roman law courts; but it was not just in terms of ceremonial that the Church drew on them. The Roman court was to the Christian a token of the Augustan peace into which our Lord was born; a symbol of justice and of the imperial rule of law to which St Paul, for instance, appealed with confidence. The background of Roman legal practice, the basilica, became one of the models for the church building. The judge sitting among his assessors and assistants in the apse of the basilica was transformed into the bishop on his throne surrounded by his presbyters, which to a Christian was a figure of Christ surrounded by his disciples. The incense altar which in the Roman law court stood in front of the judge and on which offerings of incense were made at the beginning of legal proceedings, became the Christian altar. This, too, had a curious pattern of association since it was the refusal to sacrifice incense on the basilican altar which so often marked the Christian during the Roman persecutions and led to his martyrdom. There was, therefore, almost an element of irony in the transformation of the incense altar of the pagan courts into the sacrificing table of the Christian liturgy. The crowd of postulants and spectators which gathered round and watched the legal proceedings became the body of Christian worshippers and the galleried side walks of the basilica, in which lawyers and clients could perambulate while negotiating their business, became the province of those worshippers who had no very active part to play in the liturgy.

The basilica was not the only one of the ancient forms of building which influenced the church. True, the pagan temple itself could not exercise a very strong influence; of its very nature Christian worship was different from pagan. In the Christian church the community worshipped, the community in union with its shepherd, Christ, whose presence was made visible through his surrogate, the bishop. The pagan temple was never a building for such an assembly but was the home of deity. When the gates of the temple were open the worshippers could sometimes see the statue of the god in the dimly lit temple interior as they made their sacrifices and recited their prayers at the altar at the foot of the temple steps, but on the whole it was only the priests who entered the temple. The temple building was considered as something with a secret, a mysterious interior or a public "face" to the outside. Even the Jewish Temple in Jerusalem had something in common with these pagan buildings; however, God's presence with his people was not guaranteed by any figure or image but by the inscribed tables of the law, the word of God; so that the Christian sanctuary, in so far as it was a temple, recalled in some way the holy of holies, in the Temple of Jerusalem, whose fall our Lord had foretold.

If there was a kind of religious building common in the ancient world in which Christians found elements which they could use in their churches, it was the hall of mysteries. Mystery religions became increasingly common throughout the ancient world after the year 350 B.C., after Alexander the Great. These were the religions concerned primarily with death and resurrection and the fate of the individual soul. One of the most ancient and famous of these mystery religions was centred on the shrine of Demeter at Elusis outside Athens, but there were other more popular cults like the Orphic mysteries and those of Mithras; this last cult—which originated in Persia—was particularly popular with Roman soldiers who carried it to all the provinces of the Empire. There is indeed a direct connection between the Christian church and a Mithraic temple. Under the basilica of San Clemente in Rome is the reputed house of St Clement, the fourth pope, and attached to it there is just such a temple. In all the mystery religions ritual was elaborate and, as the word mystery implies, the sense of the cult was closed to the uninitiated; the secret beliefs and the formulas which opened eternal life to the believer were ceremoniously revealed to him on initiation.

The Christian Church, too, had its mysteries, but these mysteries were not private and occult; on the contrary, they were proclaimed in public: they were the formulas of the Creed and the bread and wine which were the elements of Christian sacrifice. The form of the mystery hall, the screen and the veil, the processional entrances and exits, were to be more congenial to practices of some Eastern Churches than to the more straightforward ritualistic ways of the Latins. But Latin Christians were also affected by mystery religions; with imperial persecutions, when the Church was literally driven underground, Christian religious practices were forced to share in the atmosphere generated by the mysteries. Some Oriental Churches still retain the ceremony of guarding the doors, expelling the catechumens, but it is the Western Church which was most influenced by its underground assemblies in times of persecution.

The surroundings of Rome were honeycombed by galleried passages called catacombs. The word catacomb has an obscure origin which it owes to one of the localities where an underground cemetery is entered; catacombs, usually built on private property, were something like an elaborate subway system with galleries criss-crossing at several levels and going in several directions. The walls of these passages were lined with tiles and niches for burials, four or five of them above each other; occasionally more elaborate tombs were made, particularly for martyrs. These martyrs' sarcophagi sometimes had a pull-out stone altar for eucharistic celebration. At intervals small chambers would be opened off the galleries and these certainly acted as chapels; they might be places where martyrs or bishops were buried, they might be chapels belonging to some influential family, occasionally three or four of them would occur close together and be interconnected so that they could contain a large congregation.

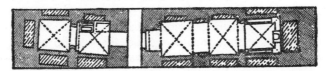

THE CHAPEL OF ST AGNES IN THE CATACOMBS

Catacomb burial originated with the Jews and certain pagan sects but became the principal form of Christian burial, and, in times of persecution, also of Christian assembly. In the end these catacombs became so extensive that if those in Rome alone were put end to end they would stretch for four hundred miles.

This form of burial and the worship associated with it made a great impression on the early Church. After the Christian religion was legalized the catacombs were restored and in places were given more opulent decoration. Pope St Damasus, late in the fourth century, was particularly enthusiastic in this work. But even in the earliest days, in the first century, catacombs were decorated; these decorations, paintings on plaster, and little enamels on thin glass mirrors or cups, are almost the first remains of Christian art. The Jewish prejudice against images had some hold on the early Church though it did not enter theological controversy until the iconoclast movement in Byzantium in the eighth century. The very poverty and sparseness of this catacomb art, the coarse bas-reliefs, the crumbling plaster, bore out the strength of the prejudice.

The first great Christian art is that of the spoken and written word.

In spite of its poverty this art was the seed of much that was to come later. The *cellae memoriae*, those chapels opening off the catacomb passages, contributed to the way in which we think of our churches. They were the tombs of the martyrs. The martyrs did not die their own death alone; but in the words of one of them, St Felicity, the African slave girl of the second century, they went to their martyrdom saying, "then Another will be in me, who will suffer for me as I will suffer for him". Other Christians saw the sufferings of the martyrs and their death as a reminder of their Saviour's death, their tortured bodies recalling the pierced body of Christ. So also the tombs of the martyrs recalled the Sepulchre in Jerusalem, and the *martyria*, the places associated with the cult of the martyr—either a chapel erected over his tomb or over the place of his martyrdom—referred the worshipper to the tomb over the original Sepulchre in Jerusalem.

In Rome, *martyria* were mostly in the catacombs or small memorial basilicas built directly over the catacombs, above the ground; but in the East they were more often small buildings constructed about two axes, that is, they had a plan consisting of some regular geometrical figure such as a square, a hexagon, an octagon or a circle. In Rome and Naples the catacombs were extremely important; in the first centuries of the Church, the usual place for the celebration of the Eucharist, however, was a large room in a private house, and a large proportion of the first churches—that is of the rooms permanently adapted for eucharistic celebration—must have been just such chapels. Not unnaturally, therefore, some scholars have thought that the arrangement of the main room of a Roman house provided the prototype for the planning of primitive churches. On the surface this is plausible enough. A large open room with an altar of the household gods in a niche at one end called the *tablinium* in which the family fire

burnt on the holy hearth and the family papers were kept
in a special safe; in front of it the seat of honour of the
head of the family; between the seat and the pool in the
floor of the room—in Roman houses there was usually an
opening in the roof over the middle of this principal room,
the atrium, and rainwater coming through was collected in
a decorative pool sunk in the floor—stood an unattached
stone altar which was in fact nothing else than an elaborate
meat chopping block. On either side of the atrium were the
alae or wings which contained the portraits—either painted
or sculptured—of the family ancestors. The arrangement of
a Greek house was slightly different, but some features
were common in both: the importance of the hearth and
the seat of the head of the family, for instance. It is these
features which some have seen reflected in basilican
churches: the apse with its mosaic, and the bishop's seat
below, referring to the *tablinium*; the altar under its
canopy between the bishop and the congregation as the
chopping block, and the transepts on either side of the
chancel—which often contained relic altars—as derived
from the *alae*. Equally the frieze of bishops' portraits
running round the church, such as the famous frieze of
popes at St Paul's outside the Walls in Rome, was also
seen as a public expression of the Roman family portraits
in the *alae*.

The trouble with this simple account, and some of the
others I have mentioned, of the origins of the Christian
church is that nothing as complex as the "essential" or
"typical" Christian church can be derived from any *one*
other kind of earlier building, in the same way as the
liturgy, which the churches were devised to shelter, drew
on a number of familiar outward forms and practices
current in the world at the time. In fact it is not very easy
to describe a typical Christian church of those early ages
since there was never any architectural uniformity in the
Church any more than there was liturgical uniformity. It is
only in Constantine's day that the great Councils made an

attempt to control liturgical use. And these attempts were more to set up liturgical norms than to impose a uniform use from outside. Even much later at the time of Charlemagne every major European see had its own separate use. Certainly most of them had their liturgical peculiarities. In England alone, after the Norman conquest, there were two main liturgical groups depending on Salisbury and York, and the imposition of the local Roman rite on practically all Latin Christianity was not accomplished until the Council of Trent in the sixteenth century. It seems to me, then, that any attempt to derive a "typical" Christian church from a single precedent is doomed to failure. Of the various elements I mentioned all probably contributed in some small measure to the form of Christian worship and to the architecture which was to enclose it: and there were other elements, too, like the philosophy schools, for instance, in which the kind of chair which was to become the bishop's throne appeared to have been given its final form, or the Jewish synagogues, in exile, where the pulpit and ambo appear for the first time.

Both in the Western and the Eastern sections of the Empire and in the countries further east in Persia, Osrhoene and Armenia, the fragile and threadbare beginnings of a Christian art were peripheral to a spectacle of Imperial opulence and pagan display demonstrated in vast and elaborate buildings. From the beginning the Christians had at any rate to agree on a negative idea of what their church was not. From the first it was conceived as something quite different from a pagan temple though it had that much in common with it that both were considered the house of god. In pagan religion this was true in the most literal sense: the temple was the god's private home where he lived, present through an image or object associated with him. But I have pointed out the difference between the Christian and the pagan act of worship. God's presence among the new Israel was not like that of one of the Olympic gods in his shrine. There was however a new

kind of temple in the Hellenistic world—the audience hall
of the Hellenistic palace, where the ruler, deified in his
lifetime, was a living presence confronting his subjects.
And here the Church did have something to learn.

Though it was a temple the church was not just an
assembly hall since it was a house of God. In this it
differed from the Jewish synagogue or the pagan court of
law with which it had other connections, as it did with the
assembly halls of the mystery religions. The artists who
built the first churches were not necessarily very profound
or startlingly original; nor was there any need for them to
be this, though no doubt some of them were artists of great
ability, but their duty was not that of creating completely
original forms. They had, on the contrary, to transform
and sanctify for Christian use forms that they had inherited
from their immediate predecessors. So it happened that the
earliest churches were something of a conflation of various
elements taken—not at random but as they seemed suitable
and relevant—from the mystery hall, the throne room, the
tomb chamber, the court of law and the family dining
room. This amalgam was differently compounded in different parts of the world. Variations were often due to climate
or building technique or local custom. More important,
they may have been due to a local development of theology
or philosophy leading to a shift of emphasis in worship, or
again they may have been due to the way in which the
relation between architectural forms and theological thinking was moving. In the course of this book I shall try to
show how some of these changes occurred and at the end
to relate them to the present needs of the Church.

CHAPTER I

FROM PENTECOST TO NICAEA

From the outset the Church was a missionary body. In his travels St Paul visited existing Christian communities in Asia Minor and Greece, on Mediterranean islands and in Italy; at the same time Christian missionaries were entering Mesopotamia, Egypt, Persia and Armenia. If legend is to be believed the gospel was first preached in India by the apostle St Thomas himself, who landed on the coast of Malabar.

Within the matter of two or three generations there were Christians around the Mediterranean basin, in the Near and Middle East, in France, and soon after that in Britain. Within two centuries Christian missionaries probably reached China.

The Christian religion spread, in the first place, inside the bounds of the Roman Empire and its confederate States. Although Church authorities counted on civil stability, guaranteed by the Pax Romana, yet the Church within the Empire, even when it was not persecuted actively, was treated by most Roman Emperors before Constantine the Great (238–337) as a religion whose public worship was not to be encouraged—what the Romans called *religio illicita*; this meant that much early Christian worship took place in secret or at any rate in private. At first, no doubt, these meetings for worship were impromptu; but soon the demands of the community suggested alterations to the room to adapt it for worship. Not unnaturally very few such house churches survive and practically none in a recognizable form. The best known is the house of St Clement in Rome which I mentioned above; perhaps the earliest and certainly the most complete is the one found some thirty years ago in the Seleucid town, Dura Europos, on the Euphrates between Aleppo and Baghdad. Dura was a caravan centre and became prosperous about 100 B.C., was seized by the Romans in A.D. 165 and fell to the Persians in the year 265, after which it declined and finally was buried by the desert sands. The Dura church, therefore, is an authentic example of a house church from the period of the persecutions. It is, in fact, a normal Syrian courtyard house slightly adapted; the largest room has been made into a Eucharist chamber with what appears to have been a small sacristy with a relic shrine room at one end, while at the entrance of the house a small room has been reserved for baptism. This primitive baptistery already has a masonry baptismal font under a fairly elaborate canopy.

Even in this poor and provincial example it is clear that the sacraments of Eucharist and baptism are given separate chambers and that each chamber is a public one. The Eucharist primarily, and to a lesser degree, baptism, confirmation, marriage and ordination were public acts of the Christian community. Baptism certainly, and at times confirmation, required special physical equipment and were housed in separate rooms; in many early churches in Africa, Greece or Asia Minor, there are not only baptisteries as at Dura, but also rooms called *chrismaria* (anointing rooms). They are practically always associated with the baptistery as baptism was clearly associated with confirmation.

It is also worth noting that some early baptisteries (as Djemila, Hippo, Timgad in North Africa, at Gerasa in Syria, at Fréjus in the South of France) appear in association with public baths or at any rate near a bath. The association of spiritual and bodily purification was very common in the early Church. Later, I shall have occasion to refer to fonts of spring water for worshippers to use before entering the church; our holy water stoups are an abbreviated and impoverished version of more generous early days. Though many Christians in those early days worshipped in a room set aside in a private house, or in adapted houses (such as the one at Dura which I described above), buildings entirely designed for Christian worship also appear at this time. These are to be found already in the second century, although as far as we know, no such building has survived into our own times. Still, in Arbela and Edessa (both in Syria), for instance, there were churches before A.D. 200. Sixty or seventy years later Gregory the Illuminator, apostle to the Armenians, ordered the building of three basilicas at Etchmiadzin, the capital of Armenia. In Rome itself, by the time of the last great Imperial persecution, that of Diocletian (305–12), there appeared to have been more than forty basilicas consecrated to Christian worship. During this persecution many churches were destroyed. At the Emperor's eastern capital, Nicomedia, was a permanent building visible from the palace windows; it could not be burnt and it had to be pulled down with great care as it adjoined several inhabited houses. But many buildings not touched by Imperial persecution also failed to survive: some because of the depredation of later persecutors—whether Moslem or pagan—others because as they deteriorated with time they were replaced by larger and more elaborate structures on the same site. The most solidly Christian part of the world at this time, Asia Minor, now equally solidly Moslem, once contained the largest number of primitive churches. The archaeologists have only made intermittent attempts to investigate the forms of these primitive buildings, but it seems at the moment as if there were several buildings of an unusual type there—small basilicas with an entrance on the long, not the short, side of the hall—and an apse opening off the other long side opposite the main entrance. The way in which this type of building relates to further developments is not at all clear yet.

There is another type of building which appears in these early centuries—mostly in Africa and Greece—which again does not relate to later developments in any obvious way, and that is the hypethral basilica, a basilican planned building with colonnades, transept and apse, but a nave without a roof. In effect, this is a long paved piece of colonnaded ground—a colonnaded court, in fact—with one large arch leading to a niche in one of the narrow sides. It is a type of building which recalls certain earlier official constructions in various provincial cities of the Empire which were chiefly concerned with commemorating the divinity of the Emperor, and in turn related back to a type of basilica found in Rome in Republican times. Under the main arch of these buildings, in front of the apse, there sometimes appeared a tomb; most of these open basilicas seem to have been funerary or memorial. It is thought that the tomb also acted as a table on which the memorial meal, an important feature of the cult of the deity in antiquity and in the early days of the Church, could be eaten. The roofless basilicas and the *cellae memoriae*, mentioned above, point to the funerary element in the development of the liturgy, an element still present in the prayers for the faithful departed recited at every Mass. It is worth pointing out again that it was one form of rite among several others. Thus the two kinds of memorial structures I have mentioned, as well as the tombs of the martyrs in the catacombs, could be expected to contribute one element among others in the formation of the Christian church building. In my view, it is fruitless to look for a single constituent element to which all church building can be referred. Anything as complex, rich and varied as the liturgy and the building which sheltered it, could not be derived from a single precedent.

In one respect the influence of these memorial structures was important in that they led to the adoption of stone as the obvious material for the construction of altars. In this matter, as in most others, there was little uniformity in the early Church, altars could be made of metal, bronze, silver or gold, various woods, rarely of ivory. Quite late in this period in the fourth century, we hear of a bishop beaten by his fractious flock with panels torn from an altar: these were presumably wooden panels. Increasingly, however, stone became the material of which altars were to be built; and indeed a number of canons were drawn up at various Councils formalizing this position.

To return to the hypethral basilica: the great difficulty in considering it as an ancestor of the Christian church is that a large colonnaded courtyard had, from its earliest days, been an appurtenance of the Christian church. Even the house church at Dura included a courtyard and some form of atrium was usual in churches of different types. In the basilica erected by St Cassian (360–435) over the body of St Victor at Marseilles the atrium was larger than the church proper and many other instances of churches associated with atria will appear in other connections.

To see quite how these elements are related I should like to consider now how the norms of church architecture came to be set once the Church came out of hiding. The decisive event of this episode is usually taken to be the Emperor Constantine's defeat of the army of his co-emperor and father-in-law, Maxentius, at the Milvian

Bridge outside Rome in the year 312. Constantine claimed to have won this battle as a result of placing the Xi-Ro monogram, which had been used as a secret sign by Christians, on the banners of his army—a decision he took as a result of a vision vouchsafed to him on the night before the battle. He did not become a Christian himself immediately but turned to a form of worship of the invincible sun, the religion favoured by his family, into which he gradually introduced Christian elements until he confessed himself a Christian; he was finally baptized on his deathbed by a heretical bishop. Nevertheless, when he met his co-emperor, Licinus, in Milan in 313, religious toleration was extended towards Christians, though with an anti-heretical rider. In 330 he revived the ancient Greek colony of Byzantium and gave it his own name; as Constantinople it became the capital of the Eastern part of the Empire. During the period when there was no Emperor in the West (465–800) it was *the* Imperial city, the undisputed capital of the Empire. It became the second Rome; the transference of the Imperial capital to Western Anatolia shifted the emphasis of all official Imperial patronage eastward. The old name of Constantinople, Byzantium, gave its name to a whole period in the history of art.

In the reign of Constantine there was a positive outbreak of church building, much of it encouraged by the Emperor himself. Particularly in Constantinople, in Rome and in the Holy Land, churches were built under direct Imperial protection. These Imperial churches immediately acquired enormous prestige; not only because they were an exemplar of Imperial taste to be imitated, but also because, being associated with the tombs of the greatest apostles and martyrs—St Peter and St Paul in Rome, and with the actual locations of the Gospel story, the Holy Sepulchre and the Grotto of the Nativity—they had the prestige of being the great reliquaries of the Christian religion.

Christianity is essentially a historical religion. The redemption of mankind was accomplished by a unique Saviour in a historical context. This meant that the places associated with his life, and in particular with his nativity and death, would have an irreplaceable significance to believers. By association, buildings erected over those spots would have an immeasurably higher value as models than any other building whatsoever. In the event, both the great church over the Sepulchre at Jerusalem and the church built over the Grotto of the Nativity at Bethlehem were basilicas associated with centralized churches.

Most of the later history of church architecture is a dialogue between these two types of building; it is therefore essential to describe their proper characteristics as soon as they appear to be defined: they do so in Constantine's reign.

Although the Christian basilica had many regional variants its essential features are these: it is a long hall usually preceded by a rectangular colonnaded court which is the same width as the main building so that one wall runs right round the complex of courtyard and basilica. This enclosure is one thing the Christian church may derive from the pagan temple. Most sacred building seemed to be characterized by this kind of enclosure: in fact the Greek word, *temenos*, a temple, is derived from the verb, *temno* (τεμνο) I cut, I cleave, I divide off. The idea of a space specially consecrated, of a sacred enclosure to which entry is made by stages, was also a feature of the Jewish temple at Jerusalem. As in the temple, the entry into the basilica was a graded one: you came in at the west end through a small porch cut in the enclosing wall; this admitted you into the atrium, the courtyard I have just described. Somewhere near the middle of it there was often a *cantharos* (Greek, drinking cup), a washing fountain. The most famous one in St Peter's in Rome consisted of a large bronze pine cone spouting water under an elaborate canopy. The section of the colonnade adjoining the basilica came to be known as the narthex and sometimes had a small porch opposite the main door into the church. When the church had no atrium there was often a narthex, a porch as wide as the whole building in the same place. Later it became the custom to interpose a vestibule between the atrium and church proper. The doors between atrium and church were usually as many as there were longwise divisions in the body of the church building.

If you entered by the central door you found yourself in the nave, the central space of the building. It was lined on either side by colonnades beyond which were lower aisles: usually one aisle on either side, sometimes—as at St Peter's again—two. These aisles were usually half the width of the nave and much lower. The colonnades supported the walls of the nave which rose higher than the roofs of the aisles and were pierced by windows which were the principal light source of the building. In some later basilicas there were two tiers of colonnades on either side of the nave, the lower one carrying a gallery, usually reserved for women, as at St Demetrius in Salonica. In the narrow wall opposite the entrance—the east wall—was an apse, usually semicircular and covered by a half dome opening off the main space. In some churches transepts divided the main basilica space from the apse. These were rooms set athwart the halls, sometimes projecting beyond the rectangle of the basilica but usually contained within it. When seen from outside the line of the transept-gable ran at right angles to the line of the main roof, implying that it covered a cross-shaped volume. This cruciform arrangement so plainly pointed to the identity between the church building and the crucified body of the Saviour that for centuries to come most standard church plans used the arrangement.

The interior was almost always much more sumptuous than the outside of the building implied. The altar stood on the nave side of the chord of the apse or in the transept —hardly ever in the nave. Often it stood over the tomb of a martyred saint and usually it was covered by some kind of canopy. To the east of it, as I pointed out earlier, were the clergy seats, to the west, reaching into the nave, was an enclosure of low screens about three feet high, sometimes made up of marble slabs carved in low relief where the community could afford such materials, or in wood; within these screens the lower clergy took their places and pulpits (ambos) which were attached to the enclosure served for scriptural readings. Such an arrangement survives in some Roman basilicas, as at Sta Maria in Cosmedin or at Sta Sabina. This kind of enclosure was less usual in Asia than in Greece where much more movement took place in the nave: the bishop sometimes had a throne in the middle of the church from which he would preach. To imagine the way these churches looked in the early centuries we must put the idea of a modern church in an Anglo-Saxon country out of our minds altogether. Pews or chairs were not heard of. Worshippers stood in preference to sitting or kneeling. The central space of the church was not a narrow hall between rows of seats but an open space occupying most of the nave with either a higher point at its centre for the bishop or a railed-off area for the lower clergy. In any case, the action of the liturgy was performed in the middle of the church while the worshippers stood in the aisles, the men on one side, the women on the other; or if there was a gallery (called *matroneum* or *gynaikon*) the men might be downstairs and the women in the galleries, an arrangement which is still current in Jewish synagogues.

In a Latin church this arrangement is completely obscured now: on the whole we have succeeded in confining our clergy, and therefore also liturgical action, to the chancel behind the communion rails. When occasion demands that the whole church be used, as on Holy Saturday, the liturgical movements are always terribly cramped. Orthodox churches (the Slavs in particular) have retained a much freer liturgical space, which they are therefore able to use to much greater effect.

In any case the type of centralized church is much more difficult to characterize than the basilica; in the Roman Empire they were particularly common for memorial constructions of all kinds. There were plenty of square tombs in Roman cemeteries (such as the one recently discovered at Ostia or the one below the crypt of St Peter's) and there were also memorials which united circle and square: even the cruciform plan could be found in Rome as early as the Republican period in such tombs as the mausoleum of the Scipioni. The sheer dominating bulk of the Imperial tombs (such as the mausoleum of Hadrian, now Castel Sant'Angelo) gave the centralized form of memorial cult building an importance which was literally overwhelming. Most of these bulky tombs had a solid core, however, so that they could not alone lead to any development of church architecture. But other types of building existed in Rome, associated with such semi-public constructions as baths and houses of Imperial princes, which held more important promise for future development. One such building, now commonly called the Temple of Minerva Medica, which is in reality the Nymphaeum, a fountain pavilion in the Licinian Gardens, was built early in the fourth century probably as part of a palace. From the outside it appeared to be a straightforward and slightly amorphous brick building, but the interior was a complex and dematerialized space. At ground level the building had ten sides, one of which was the entrance; of the other nine all opening into apses, four of these were open and colonnaded and five closed. This deliberately over-elaborate lower plan supported a simple drum with clerestory windows over which a mosaic dome appeared to float.

The first centralized churches are not quite so complex; for instance, Constantine's own foundation of Sta Costanza, built to house the splendid porphyry sarcophagus of his sister, was a circular building, again with a clerestory drum supporting a dome, itself in turn supported on a colonnade of coupled columns; a barrel vault spanned the circular passage between outer walls and the inner colonnade. There was also another colonnade which surrounded the building on the outside but only communicated with it through the single porch. A somewhat different type of building was the Baptistery of St John in the Lateran palace, an octagonal block enclosing a lantern of eight columns, one at each angle in two tiers, supporting a relatively shallow clerestory drum. These two buildings represent the two principal functions which centralized churches performed in the West, *martyria* and baptistery, and in both cases these centralized churches were usually associated with basilicas. The sophistication and intense complexity of buildings such as the Licinian Nymphaeum was however to reappear a century or more later in such Byzantine buildings as San Vitale, which I will discuss later. But from the time of Constantine many variations on the central building appeared all over the Empire and they were hardly ever as straightforward or geometric as Sta Costanza or the Lateran baptistery.

Fourth- to fifth-century buildings of this type involve a number of different combinations. There are such shapes as an octagon in a square (the cathedral of St George at Ezra in Transjordan) or a cruciform colonnaded hall in a square (the church of Apostles, Martyrs and Prophets at Gerasa, south of Ezra). At Bosra, further west, the cathedral was a quatrefoil of columns enclosed in a square which had been elaborately cut out. Many such centralized

churches were associated with eucharistic basilicas as were
the two Roman churches I mentioned earlier, but the
most celebrated instance of such an association was the
double church of the Holy Sepulchre founded by Bishop
Macarius of Jerusalem at the command and expense of the
Emperor Constantine. I have already remarked on the
enormous prestige the buildings associated with the "stations" in our Lord's life would have for all Christendom;
the cave at Bethlehem and the Sepulchre are the more
obvious of such "stations". In both cases there was a
centralized church built over the holy place and associated
with a basilica. We have no exact picture of the Constantine church of the Nativity—the present basilica was built
by the Emperor Justinian some two hundred years after
Constantine's church. This appears to have been a short
three-aisled basilica whose east end was not a simple apse
but a hexagonal enclosure over the cave of the Nativity; so
that the centralized portion of the church was half three-
sided apse and half a three-sided section bitten out of the
basilican church hall so that the spectator could sense the
rectangle of the basilica penetrating the regular hexagon of
the *martyrium*. The Sepulchre church at Jerusalem stood
inside a long rectangular enclosure with a curved wall at
the east end. This curve took up the exposed half of the
Anastasis rotunda over the empty tomb. This rotunda must
have looked a little like the Mosque of Omar on the
Temple Platform in Jerusalem which four centuries later
Byzantine craftsmen built for the Moslem masters of the
city in emulation of Constantine's building. Beyond the
rotunda, slightly detached from it (though perhaps connected to it by colonnades along the upper walls of the
enclosure) stood a relatively long basilica for eucharistic
worship with its apse towards the rotunda. At the square
western end of the rotunda there was the usual atrium.
Although later, as during the building of St Peter's in
Rome, there was to be a conflict between parties devoted

to centralized as against basilican church plans, in these early centuries the two types were, as I have pointed out, frequently associated. Both types of church appealed to classical precedent combined with other elements so that in the course of being adapted to Christian worship they became completely transformed.

The basilica as it had been conceived by the Romans was a space which had a rather easy-going quality as it were a sort of roofed over paved square. The colonnades allowed privacy for the people not directly involved in court business to perambulate up and down; the central space, whether roofed over or not, did not imply any particular movement; the judge and his assistants performed their business before a rather amorphous group of spectators who clustered in an easy circular group round the incense altar. Even the late Imperial basilica of Maxentius (Constantine's predecessor and father-in-law) had two apses, one in a short side, one in a long one, so that the apses which opened out of adjoining sides of the hall are at right angles to each other. All this was too indefinite for the historic associations of the volumes in the Christian basilica; the cloistered atrium with its fountain for purification (which carried an analogy to baptism since the unbaptized were not allowed much beyond it during the Eucharist); the narthex as an in-between space sheltered catechumens and public sinners during the liturgy; the nave as the central space for liturgical action representing this world, leading the visitor up to the triumphal arch beyond which he could see the hierarchical order, as of paradise. For this arrangement to be achieved the basilica had to incorporate different conflicting elements: the Hellenistic living room, the throne room of Roman provincial governors, philosophy school, the family tomb, the sodality dining room and all the various other elements discussed earlier, but these were all grafts on the clear rudimentary shape of the Roman law courts.

The transformation of the central type of building was more mysterious as its function was more diffuse. Centralized churches appear first as memorials over the site of an event—the Sepulchre and the Nativity are the cardinal instances. Baptisteries were also places where centralized planning was recalled since every baptistery recalled the place on the Jordan where our Lord was baptized and the rite could be carried out in a tiny space in a way in which the Eucharist, because of its nature, could never be.

In many cases, therefore, early churches were a complex made up of different shaped chambers, most often the centralized baptistery and the centralized *martyrium* accompanying a long basilican eucharistic hall. Sometimes centralized and basilican spaces were fused; I have already referred to one case in the church of the Nativity at Bethlehem but there were also more dramatic buildings such as the huge church of St Simon Stylites at Qualat Sema'n near Aleppo in Syria; the centralized martyrium of that church was the octagonal crossing of the building. In the middle of the octagon, which probably had a conical roof, was a circular opening; at the apex stood a column on which St Simon ended his days, alternate sides of the octagon opened into niches, the other four sides into three-aisled basilicas which made up the four arms of a cross; the eastern walls of this ended in three apses so that one arm became the usual eucharistic hall.

The kind of centralized space which early Christians exploited had appeared in certain late imperial buildings, chiefly in connection with palace architecture. They were usually buildings of regular but intricate geometric outline, based on the interpenetration of two more different geometrical forms. About the time of Constantine, or just before, the Licinian Nymphaeum developed upward. It is on this development that early Christian architects seized. The centralized room at ground level retained the Hellenistic complexities of imperial triclinia. But above this complex, often confusing and shady level, there rose a tall drum pierced by windows which admitted a quantity of sharp light into the centre of the building. This light brought into shimmering relief the concave mosaic in the dome which the drum supported. It also lit the centre of the building while the lower involved chambers were left in shade.

The very subtle and complex architecture of the late imperial period with its directionless—or at least unemphatic—spaces was pressed into the service of the Christian liturgy and theology; it was given a directional emphasis which had never been originally intended.

In fact the two types of church—centralized and basilican—were both affected in a similar way. Deliberately, though not always explicitly, a new hierarchical order was read into these forms. Once these readings of them had been articulated it was so emphasized that the original intention of the forms was transformed beyond recognition. The basilican plan became a horizontal, directional image of the Christian's place in the world: the division into atrium and basilica separated by the narthex between them, divided the world from the church but left an intermediate zone to accommodate those who were in transition between them, that is, catechumens and public sinners. Beyond this was the congregation of the faithful in the nave—the Church militant; and the clergy in the chancel—the Church triumphant. The centralized church presented a more condensed picture of the universe: at the ground level there was all the shadowy confusion of life and the flesh. Above, the simple drum brightening everything by its clear light, a light which represented the illumination of reason. Distant and shimmering was the celestial promise of spirit which hovered over the whole building in the dome.

These developments were accompanied by a perfecting of vaulting technique inside the Roman Empire. The techniques of brick and concrete vaulting which had appeared in Rome in the Republican period were greatly elaborated and perfected and the elaboration of vaulting ultimately led to the perfection of the dome. As I have implied, the vault and the dome were now required to cover spaces which were not as great as those of the early imperial baths, for instance, but which were much more intricate. It was no longer a case of covering a circular space with a dome and a rectangular one with a barrel vault. But cupolas had now to span over hexagons and decagons. The more sides there were to the plan of the building, of course, the nearer it was to a circle, the easier the transition between the ground plan and the hemisphere of the dome. In the decagonal Licinian Nymphaeum the transition is made by squinches, small arches, triangular on plan, springing just under the dome. With time and elaboration this device, which was very common throughout the Empire, came to be treated as a makeshift, as were the other methods of making such a transition—stone slabs placed across the corners of the square, for instance. The pendentive appears first as a continuous vault of circular section over a square space. There are third-century examples of this kind of building in Syria, but this exercised a very violent outward thrust and as the dome began to appear in conjunction with basilicas a method had to be devised to produce a more satisfactory structural form. The dome on pendentives is a perfect answer to this problem. The vault over the square is now divided into two parts, the lower, the pendentives, consist of four sections which rise towards each other from the corners, inscribing semi-circles at the four sides of the building. They meet in the centre of each side and between them impress a circle. On this relatively simple geometric system the hemisphere of a dome can rise relatively easily, and it is this system which became the staple of Byzantine and Renaissance building.

CHAPTER II

CHURCH BUILDING
UNDER WESTERN AND
EASTERN EMPIRE

By transferring the Imperial capital from Rome to Byzantium, the Emperor Constantine shifted the whole emphasis of Empire so that Roman art received a severe jolt. True, Constantine's decision only formalized the drift of the Imperial centre of gravity, a drift due to the growth of Roman possessions in the East; the consequences for the two cities, that Rome was to become the pope's city and Constantinople that of the court and the emperor, was not at all what Constantine had in mind.

Constantine's reign, then, marks a change in the complexion of Roman art. The orientalizing, Hellenistic tendency was already in ascendency when he came into power. The realism and rectitude of Hadrianic and even Severan art was a thing of the past. The Constantinian artists were concerned with violent emotion, twisted movement and dramatic relief. The more subtle and bland means employed by earlier Roman sculptors gave way to the schematization and sharp, coarse cutting which distinguishes the art of the new capital. This tendency was accentuated as the fourth century went on. The Roman Empire was growing too large to be held together by energy at the centre. The barbarians from north and east, who in the second century were contained by Imperial forces and fortifications and were absorbed into the Empire piecemeal, gradually reversed the situation, absorbed some of the Imperial territories and even took over large sectors of the fully developed Empire administration; so that in turn the barbarian domains became fractional political forces which the Empire could no longer digest.

The Imperial administration shrunk on itself, withdrew under pressure from Britain, and most of France and Germany, Spain, North Africa, Mesopotamia and Transjordan. The second half of the fourth and the first half of the fifth century was a time of shrinking uncertainty and of barbarian incursions. The Empire did not withdraw on Rome, however, but on Constantinople. Imperial authority had already been parcelled between two Caesars and two Augusti, each of the four resident in different parts of the Empire, in the third century. In 395, at the accession of the Emperors Arcadius and Honorius, the division between Western and Eastern Empire was finalized and eighty years later the Western Empire came to an end when the child Emperor, Romulus Augustulus, was "retired" by the barbarian prince, Odoacer, in 476; but it is often forgotten that Odoacer was not acting on his own authority as ruler of Italy but claimed authority as Vicar of the Eastern Emperor. From the deposition of Romulus Augustulus until the coronation of Charlemagne in 800 there was no Emperor in the West and the authority of the court at Constantinople as the supreme civilizing influence in the world was unchallenged. It was to remain so for several centuries after a new Western Empire had arisen. The official language of the Imperial court at the time of Constantine was Latin. The language of scripture and liturgy was Greek and Aramaic. This situation was reflected by the art and ceremonial of the early Christians.

The Constantinian move brought about the Hellenization of the Imperial court; Latin remained the official language in Constantinople for another two hundred years but Greek had become the common parlance. In the same way, although Greek remained the liturgical language of the Western Church into the fourth century, Latin was beginning to replace it slowly. Since there were hardly any liturgical books, in our sense, until about the middle of the fourth century—and even this is something we can only surmise—much of the liturgy was extempore and therefore there was no need to standardize the language, but while the liturgy remained largely Greek, Latin Christian literature appeared already in the second century. First writers, such as Justin Martyr and Minucius Felix, tended to work within the tradition of the Roman rhetorical schools and even the great controversial Fathers, such as St Augustine, appealed to Cicero as a model. The Christian poets again based themselves on classical precedent and various attempts were made to graft the Christian shoot on to the classical stock to the extent of attempting the construction of a Christian epic made up of fragments of the Aeneid taken out of context.

Without forcing the parallel, there is something similar about certain early Christian buildings in which the shell is of brick and mortar while the monolithic columns of vari-coloured marbles (which are occasionally of miscellaneous sizes; they had to be kept in line by varying the sizes of base and capital) are fragments taken out of classical buildings. The Emperor Constantine, in writing to Bishop Macarius of Jerusalem, about the church of the Holy Sepulchre, invites Macarius to say just how many columns he needed for his basilica. This treatment of columns as if they were precious and self-contained fragments of antiquity is related to the development of vaulting and walling techniques mentioned in the previous chapter.

As the brickwork and the concrete of the Romans improved so the stone-cutting techniques first coarsened and decayed.

Such developments were not uniform all over the Empire. In the Frankish dominions, that is present-day France, the Low Countries and Western Germany, the decay of stone cutting was very rapid. It was much slower in Italy while in Anatolia, and particularly in Byzantium and Constantinople, low relief carving remained a powerful art while mason's stone cutting became a much more schematic procedure than it had been previously. In Syria and Armenia, on the other hand, stone cutting remained a powerful craft until the economic decline of that part of the world after the depredations of the Persians and the Arabs.

Already, before the reign of Constantine, Christian teaching and writing concentrated around certain centres, Rome in the first place, Antioch on the Syrian coast, and Edessa somewhat further inland, and Alexandria in Egypt. These cities soon became centres for independent liturgical developments. A West Syrian liturgy grew up in Antioch and Edessa in the fourth century, though the centre of that liturgical family moved to Jerusalem in the fifth. In Alexandria, the Egyptian liturgical group, also known as that of St Mark, grew up. Both these liturgies were originally developed in Greek but were soon translated, the West Syrian one into Aramaic (the language from which Syriac was developed) the liturgy of St Mark into Coptic, a language derived from that of the ancient Egyptians. The Egyptian liturgy dominated the patriarchate of Alexandria which extended westward along the coast to Africa into Libya, and southward into Abyssinia. Both these liturgical centres were very much affected by the defection to the Monophysite heresies; the Monophysites spread from Damascus and Antioch, outward through Northern Syria to Armenia and the Caspian sea. The Nestorian centres were limited to Mesopotamia in the sixth and seventh centuries, but between the eighth and the tenth century the sect spread through Persia and Turkestan and Western Syria, where it survived in spite of occasional persecution, into the thirteenth century when the first Western Christians arrived on the Chinese coast.

Some scholars have wanted to see the centre for the development of Christian architecture and art in Northern Syria and Armenia. Although it is true that the first state to acknowledge Christianity as its official religion was the North Syrian Hellenistic Kingdom of Osrhoene, and that Armenia was largely Christian before the conversion of Constantine, there is no evidence of a well-developed independent and original architecture in Northern Syria before the sixth century; most of the buildings which we know from that part of the world belonged to a later period, to the seventh and eighth centuries. It is, on the face of it, most likely that the developments of architecture and art would either follow or run parallel to the developments of theology and liturgy; we should therefore look to Alexandria, Syria, Constantinople and Armenia for architectural developments.

That there was oriental influence there can be no doubt. Greek was the language spoken throughout the Empire and many of the Western Fathers spoke and wrote in it. Even in Lyons, the great Bishop Irenaeus wrote Greek in preference to Latin. From the time of Constantine onwards the habit of pilgrimage spread; one pilgrim, the Spanish nun, Etheria, who travelled round the holy places sometime between 414 and 416, gives us some idea of where these pilgrims went; she appears to have travelled overland visiting Caesarea in Cappadocia, and Edessa, off her main route, and then wandered from Antioch down the coast to the Holy Land, where she visited the holy places of both Old and New Testaments. From there she went to Egypt, down to the monastery of St Catherine on Mount Sinai, and on to Alexandria and the Egyptian monasteries. Pilgrims like Etheria became the patrons of builders in Western Europe and it is worth remembering here that Rome and its relics always attracted almost as many pilgrims as the Holy Land.

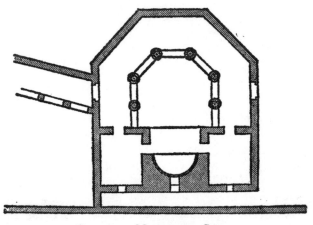

CHURCH AT MOUDJELEIA, SYRIA

In any case, whatever may have been the contribution of different centres to liturgy and theology, the organization of the Church was solidly Roman and Imperial. Constantine made all bishops members of the hierarchy of Imperial administration; and the lights and incense which are still carried before a priest as he goes into church to celebrate a high Mass are relics of the honorific lights and incense to which their official status entitled bishops. The assimilation of religious and official hierarchies is reflected in some way in the buildings produced in the Eastern

Empire during the fifth century, such as the now famous praetorium at Musmieyeh in Southern Palestine, where a traditional apsidal chamber, which presumably had a flat timber roof, was adapted to Christian use by the insertion of four columns carrying a square vault at the centre, turning the little law court into a Christian church.

The church at Musmieyeh belongs to the same manner as the Syrian churches mentioned in the previous chapter, but in Constantinople itself a new manner of looking at buildings was maturing. Nevertheless, most of the buildings of Constantine's period, and that immediately following in Constantinople, have either been replaced by later and more splendid buildings by great building Emperors like Justinian, or have been destroyed by the Turks. Of the surviving buildings of the period one of the most exciting is the tiny cruciform tomb chapel of the Empress Galla Palacidia in Ravenna, in Italy, the so-called mausoleum of Galla Palacidia, which was in reality probably a martyrium of St Lawrence, a little centralized chapel adjoining the narthex of a basilica now destroyed, whose plain unornamented brick exterior belies the fantastically rich marble and mosaic decoration of the interior. This tiny church is entirely surfaced in its lower portion with polished marbles and, above that into the vault, by brilliantly coloured mosaic, and lit through alabaster windows; the violent impact which these mosaics, on their blue ground, make on the spectator raises them far above the status of mere decoration, using the word in its derogatory sense. This building, then, marks the change implied in some of the Western buildings I have discussed, though not yet fully apparent in Syrian and Armenian architecture; in the classical world buildings were thought of as solid objects hollowed out inside; their volumes became increasingly elaborate throughout the late Imperial period until finally the situation was reversed and the building, such as this mausoleum of Galla Palacidia, became an envelope enclosing a complex volume. The comparative shabbiness of the exteriors of the fifth and sixth century buildings in Ravenna makes this change extremely obvious, particularly as these are buildings in which much of their originally elaborate and rich mosaic and marbled decoration survived, though not always as completely as in the Galla Palacidia mausoleum.

Ravenna was one of the two capitals of the Western Empire just before its dissolution: the other was Milan, and at Milan there is still surviving in a much altered form one of the most extraordinary of all the churches of this period, the centralized martyrium of St Lawrence, whose great narthex remains in the tissue of city streets as a large open square; its fabric was heavily restored after a fire at the end of the fifteenth century; of the original church there remains a tiny mosaic in the baptistery over the spot where St Ambrose probably baptized St Augustine. The church of St Lawrence is worth mentioning, even though we know very little about Milanese building of that period, because it is quite possible that much of the oriental influence which was to have such an enormous importance in the development of Frankish liturgy and church building, passed through the Milanese Imperial, and later barbarian, courts. Ravenna had a slightly different part to play. After the dissolution of the Western Empire it became the seat of Odoacer and Theodoric, the Arian Ostrogoth Kings of Italy, was retaken for the Byzantine Empire at the time of Justinian and became the seat of the Byzantine Exarch in Italy until the eighth century.

The conflict in Ravenna was not only between the Goth and the Empire but also between the Orthodox and the Arian parties; the octagonal church of San Vitale, which is perhaps the greatest achievement of Byzantine building in Western Europe and the most impressive single surviving building of this period anywhere, was conceived by its builders as a statement of the Orthodox faith against the Arian, whose octagonal baptistery has in the dome a mosaic of the adoration of the cross inspired by Arian ideas in which the figure of Christ on his throne is replaced by a jewelled cross. San Vitale is an octagonal church with an outer brick shell, each of whose side walls is pierced by three windows; the inner structure is a tall drum of eight piers which are connected on seven sides by semi-circular niches; these rise through two stories and are not composed of walls but of triple arcades whose arches are therefore two-dimensional curves. The ambulatory between the complicated outline of the niches and the straight octagon of the outside walls is spanned by a groin vault, and the niches are covered by half-domes. The eighth side opens on to a spectacularly mosaiced apse containing the altar which thrusts through the ambulatory. Above it in a half dome is the figure of Christ in glory and below him, on either side the Emperor Justinian (reigned 527–65) and his Empress Theodora, who are shown participating in an offertory procession, the Emperor carrying a paten, the Empress a chalice, while the arcaded walls of the chancel are decorated with images of eucharistic types: the sacrifice of Abel, the meal of Abraham with his angel guests, Moses striking water from the rock and the sacrifice of Melchisedech.

The central drum is roofed by a brilliantly splendid true dome constructed of rows of amphorae fitted into each other and encased in cement: a form of construction which was favoured by some later Byzantine builders and was rediscovered in the eighteenth century by architects looking for fireproof construction, such as Sir John Soane.

The architect of San Vitale is one of the first church builders whose name we know: Julianus Argentarius. Although we do not yet know whether he actually designed the building or was merely in charge of its construction, from this time onwards as the buildings became bigger and more splendid so also the names of the architects began to appear with greater frequency.

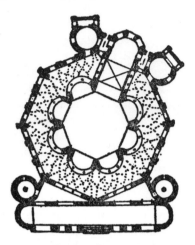

CHURCH OF SAN VITALE, RAVENNA

The complexity and richness of San Vitale, the grand and isolated apse of the altar, imply a different attitude to the Eucharist than that which pertained in the third- and fourth-century churches. This change is marked both by the shift in sacramental theology and in the devotional writings of many of the Fathers, particularly of St Basil the Great (c. 330–79) who was popularly considered to be the author, or rather the editor, of one of the commonly used liturgical formularies. The new insistence on the sinful unworthiness of the celebrant and the community, as opposed to the blinding majesty of the eucharistic Presence, is reflected not only in the words of the liturgy but within the matter of some years in the architecture of the church. St Basil's championship of the Catholic doctrine of the divinity of the Son against the Arian insistence on his humanity, is as relevant to the development of liturgy as it is to the architectural forms of San Vitale. As I have already pointed out, San Vitale is the great statement at Ravenna of Catholic doctrine against the Arians.

The court at Ravenna and its art was in all probability very dependent on Constantinople. We know relatively little of the architectural developments between the death of Constantine and the election of Justinian in 527. During his reign (he died in 565) Justinian carried out the biggest church building programme of any ruler to date, including Constantine. His patronage extended from Ravenna to Jerusalem but his greatest buildings were those in Constantinople. His churches are mostly of the type which has been mentioned in connection with Syria, that is they are conflations of basilican and centralized buildings. The simplest of these is the church of St Irene. When you look at a plan of St Irene you see a basilica whose colonnades are interrupted by two groups of piers. When, however, the building is projected into the third dimension it is seen that from these piers rise heavy arches which in turn support two domes, the one nearer the entrance rising directly on the pendentives, the one over the centre of the church rising on a drum pierced with windows. The church has an apse of the same kind as most of the early Christian churches. A more complex volume is the slightly earlier church of SS. Sergius and Bacchus; but its conversion into a mosque leaves one with very little idea of the interior feel of the building. It is, on plan, analogous but not quite as complex, as San Vitale. Again, the inner drum which bears the dome is an octagonal structure supported on eight huge piers, but here the intervals between piers which are filled with triple colonnades like San Vitale, alternate niches and straight sides. The eighth side, opening on to a chancel and an apse, is not colonnaded; the octagonal structure is set inside a square; but although this is geometrically a centralized building, yet the interior gives the impression of a long space.

This ambiguity is even more emphatically conveyed by the greatest of all Byzantine churches, the church of the Holy Wisdom in Constantinople, which was built between 532 and 537 by Justinian and restored after an earthquake between 558 and 563. The architects of S. Sophia were Anthemius of Tralles and Isidore of Miletus. Anthemius and Isidore are much more real figures than Julianus of San Vitale, particularly Anthemius who seems to have been the principal designer of the building and had a great reputation, both as a mathematician with a particular interest in applied geometry and elementary mechanics, and as a painter. Since he seemed to have a particular interest in the effects of light, the strange and interesting play of light inside S. Sophia, however marred by later alterations, should to some degree be taken as a deliberate achievement of Anthemius and not a happy accident. Isidore of Miletus, who was associated with Anthemius and had succeeded him as architect to the building of S. Sophia, was known as a mathematician and added a fifteenth book to the fourteen of Euclid: it was he who rebuilt the dome of S. Sophia after its collapse in the earthquake of 558.

S. Sophia adjoined the Imperial palace in Constantinople and was the place where the Emperor worshipped publicly. It was known in the Orthodox world simply as the Great Church in the same way as the monasteries of Mount Athos in Northern Greece are known as the Holy Mountain. This axis between the Imperial cathedral and the monastic village established a norm for the Eastern liturgy and the Orthodox euchologion states that it is setting out the divine liturgy according to St John Chrysostom and St Basil the Great as it is celebrated in the Great Church and on the Holy Mountain.

The basic shape of S. Sophia is not unlike that of SS. Sergius and Bacchus though it is a very much bigger

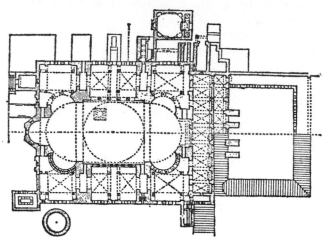

CHURCH OF S. SOPHIA, CONSTANTINOPLE

building. At the centre there is a square of four piers supporting the pendentives of the dome. The square opens on
to two huge apses on either side, covered by half domes.
These in turn open again into three smaller apses (one of
these is suppressed, being the entrance to the church and
is, as it were, flattened out against the exo-narthex). The
building was entered through a large atrium with a central
fountain. The colonnade nearest the church was double
storeyed and four huge buttresses carrying equestrian
statues project into the atrium; there was a narthex and
exo-narthex, both of which were darkish and low, through
which one entered the church proper; even as it is now,
emptied of all the silver and marble, and deprived of all
the natural articulations of the space which the Christian
liturgy requires, it is an overwhelming building. The his-
torian Procopius of Caesarea, was convinced that everyone
who visited the church felt that his heart was lifted up to
God and he said that this happened not only when he

visited it for the first time; everyone gained the same impression, as if each visit was his first.

This overwhelming impression was made on impact
rather than conveyed through an elaborate iconographical
scheme; although the decorations of the church no doubt
fit into the iconographical pattern which was to become so
tight and elaborate after the iconoclastic controversy, both
in the East and in the West. The person entering must have
been struck by the diversity of colour in the column drums,
some of which are porphyry monoliths, by the creamy
marbles and the shrine of silver—the iconostasis seems to
have been largely white marble and *repoussé* silver—and
by the brilliant mosaics in which green and red, but particularly green, appear to have been the dominating colours.
Rather inarticulately, the rhetorician Paulus Silentiarius,
writes of the surfaces in the church, "spring green from
Karyostes and many coloured Phrygians, while red and
silver shine like stars, porphyry is patterned like stars,
crocus glisten like gold, milk is poured on black flesh, blue
cornflowers grow among drifts of fallen snow".

In structural terms S. Sophia is again a rectangle, nearly
a square, broken only by the projection of the chancel
apse; then there is an internal volume composed of a cube
covered by a dome on a shallow drum from which on two
opposing sides two semi-circular niches project and which
is bound to the internal walls by four huge arches at the
angles of a continuous arcade vault all round at two levels.
Again, therefore, there is interplay between the arched
rectangle of the containing structure and the moving shiny
shadowy play of the elaborate screens; however simple the
iconography of the mosaic's elevation—and it is worth
pointing out that the marble shafting of S. Sophia rises
above the height of the martyrium, so the proportion of
mosaic to marble surfaces is unusually low when compared
with past iconoclast churches—the deliberate intensity of
the structural elaboration and the careful ambiguities of

the volume, as well as the sheer size of the structure, impressed the spectator that he was really looking on one of the great wonders of the world. The form of building which appears in SS. Sergius and Bacchus, and to much greater effect in S. Sophia, reflects, among other things a new tendency in cosmology. In his Christian topography Cosmos Indicopleustes describes the universe as a house-shaped building, that is, a rectangular oblong block covered, according to the miniatures in his book, either by a vault or by a system of domes such as at S. Sophia. The great Imperial church, therefore, is again an exemplar cosmic model as well as a commemoration of the matured eucharistic theology of the Cappadocian Fathers to which Justinian's ambition gave a unique physical reality.

One more church of Justinian's had an enormous effect on later Christian architecture, the church of the Holy Apostles. This was completely destroyed by the Turks: but its plan is reflected in such major monuments as St Mark's in Venice and the great Romanesque church of St Front at Périgueux. The church of the Holy Apostles was a cruciform building roofed over by five domes—one at the centre and one at each arm. It was a complex martyrium since it sheltered relics of all the twelve apostles. It was also a *cella memoriae* since it contained the Imperial graves *ad sanctum*.

The cult of relics and the cult of icons are parallel developments, reflections of the doctrine of the Incarnation. In the Byzantine Empire where court hierarchy and ceremonial set the whole pattern of society, the exact position of pictures in relation to each other became a matter of great importance, and as a chthonic reflection of this order, burial nearest the relics of martyrs became a question of holy precedence. But the consequences of this cult were to have a much more violent repercussion on the architecture of the Western Church than they had in the East.

The fantastic splendour of S. Sophia, the marbles inlaid with silver and ivory, the gold vessels and the green and white marble columns between nave and sanctuary, all that grandeur was never really repeated nor its scale emulated. The great economic expansion which continued for the next hundred years, or thereabouts, depended on Mediterranean trade and on the overland routes from the Orient. The first was destroyed by the rise of the Arabs and the Moslem expansion which started and gathered momentum within a hundred years of Justinian's death, the second, which was constantly menaced by personal ambitions, was disorganized by the Turkish and Mongol invasions and the grandeur of Constantinople, as well as its prosperity, was threatened by a rival port, Venice, which used the ardour and the ambition of the Crusaders to sack the Imperial city. The great bronze horses outside St Mark's and the huge Byzantine altar and reredos of beaten gold, pearls and enamels, are a humbling reminder to the West of that discreditable episode in the history of Western Christianity whose memory across eight hundred years still dulls the desire for union among Eastern Christians.

The Empire, however, did not only have trouble in the East. In the West the Gothic invaders were succeeded by another barbarian wave, the Tartar Huns and Avars and then the Slavs. The Lombards moved down to Italy before the Slavs (they will reappear in Chapter V). The Avars threatened the Empire but were ambitious beyond their power and lost their Empire to the Franks, the Germans and the Slavs. The Slavs started moving into Europe in the sixth century and soon established themselves in the Balkans with incursions into Greece and had soon occupied the bulk of the territory to the north which is now covered by Czechoslovakia, Poland and Russia. This huge territory, and the people who inhabited it, at once attracted missionaries. The brothers Cyril and Methodius, Thessolonian Greeks, set out to preach the Gospel and translated both the Scriptures and the liturgy into the old Slavonic tongue. Although they received papal approval at first, after the death of Cyril in Rome in 869, German missionaries joined the papacy against the Byzantine Slavonic movement and although Methodius ultimately received papal approval for his Slavonic liturgy, the Slav countries remained a territory divided between the Latin and the Byzantine missionaries. The quarrel over the Slavs between Rome and Constantinople became a permanent division. The old Bulgarian Empire which covered much of Serbia, Slovakia and Bulgaria, Moravia, the Ukraine or Kiev Russ as it was then called, Russia, sided with Constantinople; Croatia, Bohemia, and finally Poland, somewhat later accepted the Gospel in Latin from Rome. The division was between those who used the Latin and those who used the Cyrillic alphabet.

The economic decline in the Empire resulted in a decline in building activity; the artistic issue which moved everyone in the Empire, however, was the status and functions of icons. In the seventh century the icon had become an object of veneration of unprecedented kind; at the same time began the attack on icon worship supported in part by the Emperors, the army, a certain faction of the parish clergy and bishops. The question became a political one in Constantinople. It should be made clear here that this was not an attack on religious art in general, like that of some Protestant reformers, but specifically on the images of our Lord, our Lady and the saints, designed to receive veneration or worship. But iconoclast Emperors were again patrons of building and all the representations of the saints and martyrs were replaced by symbolical compositions, the cross, landscapes, flowers and those birds like the dove and the peacock which had always had a place in Christian iconography. Against the iconoclasts the monks stood for image worship, supported in this matter by the people and the distant authority of Rome. The iconoclast controversy lasted from the end of the seventh century until the middle of the ninth. In the meanwhile, as the Byzantine Empire grew more compressed and withdrawn on itself, so the form of the churches became more compressed and compartmented and also more elaborate. Whereas the churches of Justinian's reign were still halls where the horizontal movement was of paramount importance, the churches of the iconoclast period and of the revival which followed, are both more constrained in their volume and much more emphatic vertically. It is now the vertical space under the dome which is the dominant element in the church. With the end of the iconoclast controversy the worship of icons was re-affirmed and their hierarchical relationship defined in extreme courtly detail, depending usually on the Pantocrator in the dome from which a hierarchy of images descend down to the marble dado, with an independent group of images just beyond the central space, facing the entering visitor, on the iconostasis, or picture stand, which had now become an opaque screen between the lay worshipper and the sanctuary. The Constantinople churches of this period are mostly destroyed, such as the new church of the Emperor Basil the Macedonian, and those that have survived such as St Mary Pammaakaristes, a much later building, have lost all their decorations. The fourteenth-century frescoes in the church of the Chora survive but they already belong to another period and the best example of the flowering of icons after the victory of the iconodules are the two monastic churches near Athens, the convent at Daphne and the churches of St Luke and the Virgin at Stiris, both of the eleventh century. It is at this moment of constricted flowering that Byzantine Christianity expands beyond its frontiers into the Slav Balkans, into Russia and into Southern Italy, so making contact once again with the Goths, who as Normans had become the rulers of the Western Imperial land in Italy, and as Vikings, the masters of the Volga and Dnieper.

CHAPTER III

CHURCHES OF THE

CHRISTIAN EAST

When Bishop Polycarp of Smyrna visited Rome about the year 155 Pope Anicetus as a matter of course invited him to celebrate the Eucharist. There was at that time no question of difference in liturgical celebration or language. When Rabban Sâwmâ, the Nestorian monk from China, on an embassy to the West, celebrated a Sunday Eucharist before Nicholas IV in St Peter's the people were astonished, he tells us himself, and cried out, "the language is different, but the rite is the same".

Allowing for excessive Roman politeness it would still be true that the basic structure of the Eucharist remained similar throughout the Christian world and that in a thousand years, between Anicetus and Nicholas IV, changes were more in the externals and accidents of the rite than in its formal structure. Anicetus and Polycarp both expected the liturgy to be celebrated in Greek—the Roman might interject an occasional Latin vernacular prayer. Sâwmâ celebrated his liturgy in Syriac, a derivative of Aramaic, with insertions in Mongolian, but as with his Latin contemporaries and all churchmen, Orthodox, Catholic or Protestant, the celebration of the Eucharist contained chants and scriptural readings; some form of offertory, followed by the anaphora which included the words of the institution; communion and dismissal concluded the service. This sequence of liturgical elements was formulated first in Greek by Greek-speaking Christians and, as I have pointed out, developed differently in different parts of the world until in modern times the basic form has become so overladen with accretions that the basic unity of different rites would never be apparent to the uninstructed spectator. In the same way, the Christian altar which, with the development of the liturgy and eucharistic devotion, acquired a canopy on columns and was veiled with curtains, just as the figure of the Emperor or Empress appears veiled in diptych panels, has also been transformed in different ways so that its origins are no longer obvious.

In the West it is usually a long stone box, sometimes twelve or fifteen feet long, usually attached to the east wall of the chancel surmounted by shelves carrying candlesticks and flowers; there is often a huge altarpiece above, while the veils of antiquity have been atrophied to side curtains or valences which only appear on mock medieval altars. In the East the altar is more usually a cube or near cube, usually concealed behind a solid screen covered with icons of our Lord and the saints. The screen usually has three doors and through these doors the Gospel and the eucharistic elements are carried in procession. The "typical" plan of an Orthodox church is a trifoliate cross-in-square; this means that the church is rectangular or square, the four piers in the middle supporting a dome over the centre with barrel vaults joining the piers to the outside walls and the four left-over squares covered, according to the means of the church builders, with domes, groin vaults, barrels or just a sloping roof. The east wall opens into three apses of which the central one contains the sanctuary, the one on the left, the prothesis, the one on the right, the diakonikon. The diakonikon is a repository for the archives and vessels

of the church, for relics and the movable icons, the prothesis is used for the preparation of the eucharistic elements
and, when it is large enough, for the processions to form.
Orthodox churches did not contain the multitude of
chapels and altars usual in the West. This kind of division
was, like the rest of Orthodox ceremonial, given its formu-
lation just after the iconoclast period. The Slav-speaking
Orthodox took over the Byzantine liturgy in the form I
have described as well as the ideas of Empire current in
Byzantium.

First the ruler of the Bulgarians, and then the much
more powerful and sophisticated King of the Serbians,
adopted the title of Emperor and claimed independence
for the national church. The Serbian Empire, under Tsar
Dušan (1331–5) marked the climax of Balkan Slav Christianity. Stephen Dušan was the first Balkan prince to call
himself Emperor and autocrat, and the first to sport the
double-headed eagle as his badge. He was able to humiliate
the Imperial forces and keep the Turks at bay; but soon
after his death the Turks broke the Serbian Empire in 1389
at Koosovo and the rump Serbian state only survived six
years after the fall of Constantinople when it was absorbed
into the Ottoman Empire. While the Bulgarians were
always completely dependent on Constantinople the
Serbians were both more independent of the Imperial
court and more enterprising. Occasionally, Western architects were employed there; particularly Italians, such as
the Franciscan Vita, who built the monastery of Decani in
the middle of the fourteenth century in a strange white and
pink Pisan Byzantine style. But in fact the Serbians did not
depart far from the norms set by Constantinople even after
they had established their Church as an independent ecclesiastical unit and whose head took the title of Patriarch.

The church building of the Balkans only begins in the
ninth century, that is, when the iconoclast episode in the

Empire was definitely closed. There were of course regional differences within the peninsula. There was a marvellous flowering of late Byzantine building at Mistra, the capital of the Despots of Morfa: an architecture of thick piers and tall domes and marvellously courtly and remote fresco painting. In Serbia the rather more straightforward and ample measures of the Latin-tinged South Slavs were current, while in Bulgaria and Rumania the essential Byzantine forms are twisted and elongated. All these developments are summed up in the monastic colony of Mount Athos; here monks from all over the Orthodox world reproduce in their different monasteries the various styles of their places of origin: Syria, Anatolia, Serbia and Russia.

Since this essay deals with church building I have not so far said anything about monastic building although several of the churches so far mentioned, such as St Simon Stylites, for instance, or St Paul's outside the Walls, were in fact abbey churches. The monastic was to play an enormously important rôle in the development and transformation of Western church architecture, but in considering the buildings of Orthodoxy it will have been noticed that the rôle of the monks has so far been passive. In fact the bulk of the developments so far discussed took place in towns. The elaboration of late imperial volumes, and the rather shabby exteriors which these volumes were given, imply that this architecture was an urban one and the buildings formed part of the texture of the town so that their exteriors were a relatively unimportant matter.

Countrymen are notoriously more conservative than townspeople and the firm hold which Christianity gained in the towns was not always reflected by the surrounding countryside. The country church as a norm of a Christian building—as it is in Great Britain—is a relatively late historical phenomenon. From the seventh century onwards churches as isolated buildings in the landscape became increasingly important and the relationship between exterior and interior is changed so that now the two become equally important. This is obvious in the Balkans but will be seen more clearly in the Armenian examples; of course, this move was already implicit in the Great Eastern churches which I have mentioned in the second chapter.

While the church architecture of the Balkans inevitably fell under the direct influence of the Byzantine Empire the architecture of the Northern Slavs developed away from it and survived the fall of Constantinople by several centuries. St Vladimir, the convert Prince of Kiev, founded the cathedral of St Sofia in emulation of the great Imperial church in Kiev late in the tenth century. The late Byzantine developments were heavily marked here. It was a building whose thick piers carried thirteen small domes of which the great central one symbolized Christ, and the other twelve the apostles. Unfortunately this church has been very much altered and enlarged so that there are now very many more domes and both the original effect of the volume and the numerical symbolism has disappeared. Vladimir and his immediate successors were great builders but Kiev Russ was soon hard pressed by the Mongols, and when the Golden Horde swept through Asia into Europe Kiev Russ fell, never to regain its original political or religious importance which was taken over in the first place by Novgorod and later by Moscow.

Novgorod, which is considerably north of Kiev, modified the Byzantine architecture which they had learnt from the Ruthenians. The Princes of Novgorod and Suzdal to the east, evolved a courtly style which appeared to echo some of the Armenian achievements as much as those of Constantinople. The churches rise abruptly out of the ground as solid white buildings whose exterior is subdivided in a way which suggests the tall compartments inside. Mosaic in the interior is very rare, as in Serbia, the decorations are painted in a brilliant and rapid fresco technique while the exterior might have been heavily stylized relief ornament reminiscent of Scythian jewellery or carving. The tall constricted domed chambers which were evolved by the Byzantine builders to fit the situation of the late Empire seemed to suit the Russians of this period equally well; but while Byzantine architects never developed a formula for relating this complex volume to the exterior the Russians clearly demarcated the subdivisions of the interior on the outside walls of the building by creating blind colonnades which were an exposition of the interior order. The saucer dome on a tall drum, however, was soon found to be inadequate for Russian snow and the characteristic onion shape which we associate with Russian church architecture was developed to deal with the huge weights of snow.

The Mongols remained inside Russian territory and as a menace to the disunited Russian princes until they were

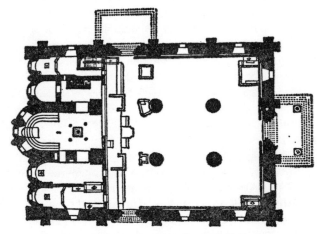

CATHEDRAL OF THE ASSUMPTION, MOSCOW

defeated in the sixteenth century by Ivan the Great, who had married a Byzantine princess twenty years after the fall of Constantinople. His nephew was Ivan the Terrible who, like Stephen Dušan in Serbia, had assumed the title of Tsar and taken the double-headed eagle for his badge.

The Orthodox Church of the north never acquired a church of either the scale or the authority of St Sophia in Constantinople. Yet it did have a definite centre in Moscow, the Russian capital, to which the Russian metropolitan had already moved from Suzdal. Moscow came to be called the third Rome. Both Ivan the Great and his nephew, Ivan the Terrible, were great builders; the three Italianate cathedrals of the Kremlin being their best-known achievement. But just outside the Kremlin walls Ivan the Terrible had built the curious church of Basil the Great in which the nine separate volumes of the cross in square actually became independent chapels so that the church is a space from which rise eight tall thin-domed individual chapels, dominated by the central conical roof of the ninth one, while their walls and domes are entirely encrusted with coarse and heavy ornament. The tall conical roof over the central space became one of the staples of Russian church building and again was better than the Byzantine dome in Russian climatic conditions; but although it marked a return to the practice of primitive church builders in Mesopotamia before the introduction of the dome, it was frowned upon by eighteenth-century conservatives who as a matter of canon law laid down that the dome is the only proper covering for the central space of the Orthodox Church.

In the nineteenth century the Russian Church remained prosperous and building activities were extensive; although there are some charming buildings of the period, particularly in timber, the cemetery church of Kishiski Posts, near Olovetz, for instance, or the much grander church of the Intercession of the Virgin at Fili near Moscow, as well as very considerable monastic building, there is very little which makes any great contribution to the development of church architecture generally; since the Revolution there has been virtually no church building in Russia and with it the direct Byzantine tradition has been extinguished.

The Armenian Church, in spite of its present dispersal throughout the world and lack of a physical centre such as Constantinople or Rome was for the Orthodox and Catholics, was one of enormous importance for the development of church architecture. The Armenians became separated from the main body of Christians after the Council of Chalcedon in 451 when they became Monophysite. Armenia had then already been partitioned between the Roman Empire and the Persians; in 519, however, more of the country came under Byzantine rule and although in the general Arab invasion of the Near East Armenia fell to them in about 700, it became an independent country again in 885 and so remained until 1046. It is true that it was at this last period that most of the Armenian buildings which we now know were built. The two important centres of the country were Etschmiatzin where the head of the Armenian Church, the Katholicos, still lives in a monastery—this is now in Russia—and Ani, the capital of the medieval kingdom which was known in its time as the city of the thousand-and-one churches. Of these, however, very few remain. But they form a coherent and sometimes brilliant corpus of buildings. There is a preponderance of centrally planned churches; a square with four apses, for instance, is fairly common and there are a great many variations on that particular formula, as for instance the church of St Hripsineh at Etschmiatzin, where the interior divisions of the building are marked on the outside by curious

triangular-shaped niches. The Armenians contributed much
to the development of church architecture; the most
obvious thing is the expression of the interior division of
the building in the panelling and ornament of the exterior;
the further development of the domed church in relation
to the vault, their brilliant masonry which created a demand for Armenian masons, both in Byzantium and in
Russia; and the development of a highly original though
somewhat barbarous sculptured ornament.

The Georgians who lived directly to the north of the
Armenians were too much under the influence of Constantinople to develop either an authentic native liturgy or
architecture, but they served as a filter for the northward
expansion of Armenian influence. This expansion was
transmitted both by travellers impressed by the splendour
of Armenian achievements and by Armenian sculptors
and stonemasons whose high reputation led to their em-
ployment in Russia and in Constantinople, particularly
during the reign of the Armenian emperors.

The contribution of Alexandria to the general development of church architecture is very difficult to estimate;
Alexandrian churches unlike those of Constantinople were
not simply altered by the modern invaders to suit their
use but were mostly destroyed or rendered unrecognizable.
We know much more about the Alexandrian element in
Christian art, particularly the Alexandrian contribution to
the course of Western painting, since innumerable en-
caustic portraits on Hellenistic mummy cases display a
development of a sophisticated and increasingly familiar-
ized school of portrait painting; while we also know that
the miniature and landscape painters of Alexandria had
far-reaching effects on the imperial ateliers in Constantinople. But Egypt's contribution to the Church was not
limited to Alexandrian sophistication: Egypt, and the
Thebaid in particular, was the fatherland of monachism;

it was in Egypt that Christian monastic life took shape and its earliest rules were formulated. The language of the Alexandrian liturgy of St Mark was Greek. In the monasteries a Coptic liturgy was developed in the fourth century. It was this liturgy which the missionary monks carried down to Abyssinia. Moslem invaders who caused the decline of the Egyptian Church, completely cut off the Coptic Christians of Abyssinia (who, in any case, had lapsed into the Monophysite heresy) from the rest of the Christian body and the Abyssinian Church developed in almost absolute isolation until the middle of the nineteenth century.

Until the Moslem conquest of Egypt Abyssinia was a relatively prosperous and powerful country at a technical and economic level far higher in its day than most of Western Europe. It had trading contacts by sea with India and China and it is partly through these contacts, perhaps, that a form of rock-cut church quite unlike anything else in the rest of the Christian world developed in Abyssinia during the early Middle Ages. These churches appear also to be related to the building practice of the Southern Arabs and sometimes imitate in detail timber forms, though they are cut out of the living rock. For the rest, Ethiopian churches are often circular of the centralized type. When, however, churches of the rectangular type are found they are usually as in Egypt subdivided most elaborately by a series of screens which separate the sanctuary from the nave and divide the nave into men's and women's parts. These screens are elaborately carved but not painted, and have none of the "icon-exhibition" character of the iconostasis of Orthodox churches, though something analogous to the Western rood screen is occasionally found. The interiors are whitewashed and stone-paved, while the screens retain the natural colour of the wood.

Of the further oriental outposts of the Church in China, Turkestan and Northern India very little is known since practically all were destroyed. The buildings in Malabar are too fragmentary and heavily restored to give us any clear idea of what an early medieval Christian architecture looked like. The outposts of oriental influence in the West, in Spain, Southern Italy and Aquitaine, belong to the sections dealing with Western architecture, as do the relations between the imperial court of the West and that of Constantinople.

CHAPTER IV

THE FLOWERING OF THE WESTERN EMPIRE

The word "church" suggests in England the image of a country parish church of the late Middle Ages; in America a nineteenth-century Gothic Revival building is probably the equivalent. The first balloon-framed church to go up in Chicago (in 1835) was a simplified version of such a European medieval chapel. But the line of development which produced the medieval church type is an eccentric branching off from the main stream of church architecture. The bulk of important early church buildings before the year 800 were built east of Italy and on the southern shores of the Mediterranean; all Western European architecture as well as the few churches that were built in the West before the fifth century are provincial products of the Roman Empire. There is a hiatus in all building in Europe while the invading barbarians, whom the crumbling Roman Empire could not absorb, slowly settled into the nation states of Western Europe; and a new church architecture appears early in the seventh century no longer directly depending on Roman imperial practice, but using the ancient themes transformed by the economic conditions and the barbarian practices of the new peoples. Partly because of this the period between the end of the

Western Empire and the reign of Charlemagne is known as the Dark Ages, but also because our knowledge of it is fragmentary and sources are very often hard to come by. One thing is clear, however: throughout this period Rome was the undisputed centre of the Western Church and it was in Rome that the liturgy was elaborated and formalized in a new way.

We do not know as yet when Latin superseded Greek as the liturgical language of the Roman Church. It had certainly done so by the sixth century and the process may have been complete in the fifth. By that time too the central section of the Mass, the canon, had assumed roughly its present form. It was the Popes Felix (483–92) and Gelasius I (492–6) who fixed the liturgy in its present form and St Gregory the Great (590–604) who reduced the ancient elements to a simpler order. It was Gregory too who sent St Augustine to England in 596. Augustine was an Italian monk who came to Britain to preach the Gospel to the English and to restore contact between the old Celtic Churches and the Roman See. There had been Christians all over Western Europe, including Britain, since the second century; three British bishops were present at the first Council of Arles (314). But the liturgical practice of Western Europe did not conform strictly to the Roman model. Western Europe was divided into two main liturgical schools during the Dark Ages, the Gallican and the Romano-African: it will be remembered that the south coast of the Mediterranean is crowded with Christian basilicas of the strict Roman kind.

While the text of the Roman liturgy became fixed, new liturgical practices were appearing (such as the custom of the processions to the station churches) which were not produced directly by the inner structure of the Mass but grew out of the impact of the changing context in which the Church acted on increasingly formalized customs. As the number of worshippers increased and the ecclesiastical organization grew, so also the financial resources of the Christian community increased; although Rome in the sixth century was a provincial city when compared with Byzantium and Constantinople, yet church buildings multiplied relatively quickly. As the Roman rite achieved its final form it became customary for the pope, as bishop of the city, to make a round of the parish churches and celebrate a liturgy in a different church on different days of importance in the Christian year. Even today we find in the Roman Missal rather meaningless references to station churches, to a custom, that is, which has become a vestige even in Rome itself. At the head of the propers of the day in Holy Week, for instance, it can be observed that Palm Sunday Mass was celebrated at St John Lateran, the pope's cathedral, on Monday at St Praxedes, Tuesday at St Prisca, Wednesday at St Mary Major, Thursday at St John Lateran again, Good Friday at the church of the Holy Cross, Saturday at St John Lateran and Easter Sunday at St Mary Major. These papal Masses have left their mark in certain atrophied customs which have persisted in the Roman rite, but they also mark the beginning of a new relationship between the Church and its environment in Western Europe. In considering Byzantine churches, I remarked on the early development of the church building as a rich and elaborate interior in contrast to the rather poor exterior. What was true of the rest of the Byzantine Empire was also true of Rome in this matter; since, in spite of the dominating influence which Rome was to exercise on the worship and theology of Western Christendom during the formative sixth and seventh centuries, it nevertheless appears to have been, in terms of architecture and fashion, a provincial outpost of Byzantium.

The stational Masses must be seen as a custom demanding a reconsideration of the church building. The custom of religious processions was familiar to the pagan Roman in general. During the era of persecutions Christians were naturally discreet in public display and since the Church was never eager to imitate pagan pomp the custom of holding religious processions grew up relatively slowly. In Byzantium religious processions were in any case subsidiary to the splendour of the imperial court. But in Rome they grew up round the figure of the city's bishop, who by then was acknowledged as a supreme arbiter of the Church, and round the great concentration of the relics of the martyrs. During the Dark Ages, therefore, the church building becomes less and less of a hall inserted into the tight texture of a Roman city and increasingly the isolated building whose internal and external arrangements have complementary functions and equal importance. Paradoxically, we know a great deal less about the development of church architecture in Western Europe during this period than we know about the equivalent period in the East. The imperial administration withdrew upon Constantinople rather than on Rome and the great crisis of Mediterranean trade which followed the emergence of Islam as a world power gave the final blow to the already declining urban organization of Western Europe. Such Western centres as Paris, Trier, London, Cologne, shrank and fell into ruins; and when these cities expanded again in a later age the rebuilding did not follow the relatively insignificant remains; more often what was there was simply used as a quarry for building materials. Archaeologists will no doubt tell us a great deal more than we already know about Christian building in the West. Even now we have a much clearer picture of what the art of the earliest Christians in this country was like before Augustine than was available fifty years ago, but we still know very little about what must have been a charming and vigorous but very provincial art.

In any case church buildings in Western Europe prior to the time of Charlemagne are very small compared to the Roman basilicas or to the Byzantine churches of the same period. But even in Rome during the Dark Ages building had practically come to a standstill and the great reforming popes of liturgical history, such as Gelasius and Gregory the Great, are remembered more as restorers of existing buildings than as builders of new ones. The last great building period in the West centred on Milan and Rome and was the result of Justinian's (483–565) activities all over the Mediterranean basin; Justinian too established a bridgehead for Byzantine influence in Western Europe at Ravenna. The earliest churches of any importance which have survived from this period in Western Europe are of extreme simplicity, such as Escomb church, Durham. Escomb is one of the few surviving fragments of Northumbrian church building, as are the crypts at Hexham and Ripon. There was, however, another centre of church building in Britain, further south, in Kent. Parts of St Martin's, Canterbury, are about the best-known surviving examples of early building of that period. The buildings in Kent were, of course, dominated by the Roman figure of St Augustine, and in Northumbria too St Benedict Biscop (c. 628–89), an influential Northumbrian monk, did his best to make Northumbrian Christians conform to Roman liturgical practice and Roman fashions in music and architecture. Although British Christendom was the outer limit of Roman influence towards the northwest it was nevertheless extremely important. It was British monks who carried their missionary activities into Northern France and to the new German peoples beyond the Rhine. Two generations later St Boniface (680–754; born in Crediton, Devon) converted Bavaria and Thuringia, reorganized the Frankish Church and died a martyr's death in Frisia; and a generation later Alcuin of York (735–

804) became the intellectual and theological arbiter of the court of Charlemagne.

In the reign of Charlemagne another period of building activity started. The ambitious Pepin the Short had displaced the decaying Merovingian dynasty. The territorial claims, the towering eminence among Western Europeans and his function as the defender of Christendom from the Germanic tribes in the East and the Moors across the Pyrenees, was recognized by the papacy in the elevation of his brilliant son to the Empire. Charlemagne was crowned in the great Roman basilica of St Peter's, by Pope Leo III on Christmas day in the year 800, as Emperor of the West, and this new status of Holy Roman Emperor was soon accepted, if not actually recognized, by the Byzantine Emperor.

Charlemagne's coronation signified that an axis had been set up between the papacy in Rome, which claimed spiritual leadership over all Christians, and its secular protector or supreme arbiter of all temporal affairs in the world, the Holy Roman Emperor, who in practice was always to be a Teutonic ruler, usually resident in Northern Europe. This axis was to dominate European affairs from the time of Charlemagne to that of Charles V (1500–58) and though its power waned after the Reformation it remained a considerable force until the abdication of the last emperor in 1804. Charlemagne's policy in ecclesiastical and cultural matters was motivated by his need to create a suitable environment for the new Imperial authority. He modelled himself on the Roman Emperor who was to become an archetype of the Christian ruler, Constantine the Great, and he aimed to make his court the centre of a new Latin culture much as the Byzantine Empire's court was the centre of a Greek one. Charlemagne's reforms, therefore, aimed at making the large independent Gallican Church, which prevailed in his domains, into a Roman and Latin one. As far as possible the Roman liturgy replaced the Gallican. The organization of imperial authority went hand in hand with an ecclesiastical division of the newly conquered pagan lands and the appointment of suitable bishops; many of them were chosen from among the English Benedictines who were very active as missionaries.

As may be expected, both Northumbrian and Kentish church building had its echo on the Continent; in the Rhine Valley mostly the Northumbrian rectangular square apse churches appeared, whereas in the old Merovingian lands there were single-cell buildings with a rounded apse and a column screen. However, most of these buildings were too simple to last for any length of time and were replaced by more ambitious structures. Occasional survivals in mountain districts, in the Pyrenees or in the Alps, show usually simple longitudinal halls, though occasionally something more ambitious, like the cross-square church with seven apses at Germigny-des-Près, did appear. This kind of echo of Byzantine planning inspired the most ambitious of Charlemagne's church buildings, like the octagonal Imperial Palatine chapel in Aachen. The Palatine chapel also relates to a number of octagonal buildings in Mediterranean lands, particularly to the church of San Vitale at Ravenna and the baptistery of Constantine by the Lateran Palace. It was itself built on the site of a Roman nymphaeum which had been replaced by a relic chapel in the days of Pepin the Short; it was deliberately conceived *more Romano* according to Charlemagne's biographer Einhard, and antique Roman columns were used in its construction. The central space was surrounded by a gallery in which, opposite the apse with its altar, the marble throne of Charlemagne was set up, so that when the church was in operation the Emperor, among his court, under the golden dome, dominated the people in the body of the building; this majestic group were proposed to the contemplation of the congregation as the early equivalent of the clergy grouped round the altar of the Saviour which faced the throne across the gallery, and under which, at the main floor level, stood the altar of the Virgin. Charlemagne was buried in this chapel, and soon afterwards it became a coronation church for German kings, some thirty of whom were crowned there. The western gallery with its throne appears to have had an enormous influence on subsequent building in Frankish and German lands and it probably in part accounts for the contrivance of the westwork. The westwork is a feature which appeared in many Carolingian churches and until the eleventh century was an important factor in European church building. It consisted of a vaulted ground floor which carried a tall gallery, the gallery in its turn being vaulted by one or more towers. It is from this that later the double apse churches seem to have developed. Very few of these westworks have survived. The most famous of the early ones are perhaps those at Corvey in Germany, and the abbey of Centula at St Riquier in France. With time the westworks became more impressive and more elaborate. At St Gertrude, Nivelle on the Meuse, begun in the year 1000, and at St Michael's in Hildesheim, begun in the same year, they are extremely prominent. A more interesting one is the Essen Munster, where the westwork deliberately repeats certain features of the Aachen Palatine chapel.

The westwork affected the general configuration of Western churches throughout the Middle Ages. It became increasingly rare after the twelfth century and in that sense had no permanent effect on Western church architecture. But the way in which it accommodated processions points to a new factor in church planning. Processions in connection with the Eucharist seem to have formed part of the earliest liturgies, and probably processions inside churches became fairly common towards the end of antiquity. The development of the stations in Rome, which I mentioned earlier, is paralleled by processional devotions in the Holy Land, in Jerusalem in particular, and the Byzantine court developed a very prominent processional ceremonial of its own. Although in Rome official processions were not at first related to the Church the new Emperor Charlemagne and the Germanic kingdoms soon developed elaborate ceremonial processions in connection with the Imperial and Royal Courts. It became a custom for the Royal Emperor to tour his dominions and be crowned by the bishops of several of the big cities. These coronations always took place in at least two churches; the actual crowning and the Mass up to the Creed in one church, after which the Emperor, the clergy and the people proceeded to another building where the Mass from the Offertory to the Dismissal was celebrated. This custom was provided for in many cities by the placing of two churches at either end of a particular avenue or market square, and the imperial custom was soon copied in the lower reaches of authority.

The development of processions affected, therefore, the disposition of church buildings inside the town as well as the layout of the actual church plan, and as we shall see later the ambulatory became an increasingly important part of the church plan. Related to the new popularity of the procession was the cult of the martyrs and their relics. As I have already pointed out, martyria and eucharistic halls were separated in the early days of the Church. It was some time after the age of Constantine that the mensa, the altar of the eucharistic hall, was required to be in contact with the "memoria" of the martyr. In Rome itself, from the seventh century onwards, relics which had been venerated in the catacombs were moved up into existing churches and quite often, at about the time of Gregory the Great, we find earlier basilican churches rededicated to mark transference of the relics. The most conspicuous example of this is the rededication of the pope's cathedral, the Constantinian basilica of the Saviour, to Saints John the Baptist and the Evangelist, some time before 870.

The great planning problem which the conflation of martyrium and eucharistic church proposed was that of allowing access to the relic to large numbers of the faithful in such a way that it might not interfere with the celebration at the high altar. As a monumental solution of this in St Peter's in Rome the altar had a higher platform placed over the presumed tomb of St Peter in the basilica, between the transept and the nave, and where the actual "memoria" was surrounded by a passage-way to which access was available at a lower level; this became a model for many later developments. The association of altar and relic is an obvious one for Christians and soon altars not associated with the martyrs became shrines to one or more of such relics so that it finally became a rule of the Church that every altar should contain a small relic shrine of one or more martyrs.

The crypt under the high altar, with its evocation of the catacomb, was a much more important and lasting influential feature of church building than the westwork. Crypt, altar and westwork suggest that before the Carolingian period the church building was already becoming fragmented. Moreover, in the eighth century, prelates were not content with uniting eucharistic hall to martyrium but now, more ambitiously, enlarged their crypts and filled them with relics in evocation of the Catacomb Lombardia. The first of such hall crypts was built in the chancel of Santa Maria in Cosmedin during the reign of Hadrian I (772–95); this filling of the crypt with relics related to another feature of Carolingian architecture. In the churches of the ninth and tenth centuries the main altar dedicated

to a martyr or a local saint was still the centre of the
church but now niches and the available subsidiary
chambers such as the westwork, were filled with secondary
altars, dedicated to other martyrs, and so the new importance of processions, on which I have remarked, was now
elaborating the church into a succession of martyr shrines,
sometimes even conceived as a representation of the stages
of the passion. We still have a relic of this development
in the Stations of the Cross, set out along the walls of a
church building, which reproduce in some sort the way
which Christ followed carrying his cross in Jerusalem.
One of the earliest drawn documents about architecture
was the ninth-century plan of the Abbey of St Gall in
east Switzerland which displays in schematic form the
conception of the church as a gathering up of the fragments from martyr shrines and pilgrimage centres of the
whole of Christendom into one building; it therefore becomes a new kind of *imago mundi*, a schematic representation of the world redeemed by the passion of Christ,
which is manifested also in the minor passions of each one
of his martyrs.

Naturally, the use of architectural quotation, on which
I commented, serves to emphasize this impression, and
while in the relatively sophisticated court architecture of
Carolingian and Ottonian times is more allusive and pic-
torial than it was to become in later and coarser times, and
at a lower level of sophistication these devices could become literal and tied to such matters as reproducing the
same number of columns or even, on the wall, the dimensions of the building which the builders wished the faithful
to remember.

The themes of westwork, of the complex martyrium, of
the relic crypt, became the staple of later medieval church
building. Although the period between Charlemagne and
Otto III therefore is not comparable with the succeeding

centuries in which, all over Europe, the great medieval cathedrals were built, it is nevertheless the time during which both theological and formal presuppositions which were to underline all medieval church building were first posited, elaborated and given some experimental expression.

Another custom, belonging to a different order of religious preoccupation, must also be mentioned here and that is the practice of burial *ad sanctum*; this means the practice which originated in the catacombs of being buried near the tomb of a martyr. This practice, although it has no real theological implications, became extremely common and with the multiplication of saints' altars private patronage of a particular saint's chapel was associated with the tomb of the founder. In earliest times these tombs, not unnaturally, clustered round the *confessio*, a crypt under the high altar chambers and accessible from the main floor level, but in the course of time and with the multiplication of altars the associations of altar and tomb became closer, leading to the disruptive abuse of chantry chapels in the high Gothic cathedrals.

The rise of the Holy Roman Empire of the tenth and eleventh centuries was paralleled by the great development of monastic life and the education of the Imperial household was carried out in the great Carolingian abbey; soon its monasteries were to provide not only the great Imperial bishops but also the occasional pope. The exclusively Latin orientation of Charlemagne's court was not to last. Inevitably even he flirted with the Eastern Empire and considered a Greek marriage, but it was Otto II who married the Byzantine princess Theophano, in 972—a marriage which led to renewed Byzantine influence on Western building and architecture. Although it is difficult to disentangle the different elements in Ottonian architecture it might be best if one took as a particular example the

church of Cyriacus in Gernrode in Saxony as indicative.
Although it was begun by a local magnate it was said to
have been finished under the influence of the Empress
Theophano herself, and it presents certain new features.
There are, of course, familiar elements—colonnaded aisles
and a wider nave, a substantial transept and westwork, as
well as a crypt below the altar. But at St Cyriacus, as in
many churches of the late tenth and eleventh centuries, the
colonnade is no longer a continuous one but is divided
into bays by thick piers. This again adds an element of
modulation to the rather straightforward space which may
owe something to the Byzantine influence. This kind of
articulation was to become increasingly important. Very
soon it was transferred to the exterior of the building and
elaborate blind arcading became a feature of late Romanesque, and later of Gothic, architecture. As time went on
the modulation of every wall surface would become the
principal ornamental device of medieval architecture.

Theophano also became the Regent of her young son
Otto III (981–1002). Like Charlemagne, Otto III was
crowned on Christmas Day and like him he relied on a
direct contact with the papacy. Following his father's example, he attempted to reduce Italy to direct Imperial
obedience and, like his father, he died in the attempt.
The classical link was not to have the enormous power it
exercised during the first two centuries of the Holy Roman
Empire for many years to come. The historicizing and epic
sophistication of the first Imperial court of the Ottonian
Emperors was contemporary with a period of apocalyptic
fear which led to a diminution of building activity as the
year 1000 approached. At the same time the growing
power of the Empire led to an ecclesiastical reaction and
a period of more troubled relationship between pope and
emperor in succeeding centuries, while the centre of the
imperial administration shifted northwards. The year 1000

marks a break which is followed by a burst of building activity. Some of the largest Romanesque churches in Europe, as St Michael at Hildesheim, St Martin at Canigou, St Gertrude at Nivelle, were begun in the first three or four years of the eleventh century. Later in the century a great spate of building activity began in Britain with the Norman conquest, but British architecture of the time came to be separated from what went on in France, and in particular in the Norman dominions of William the Conqueror.

The second half of the eleventh century was a time of rapid transformation which had a very powerful effect on European architecture. It was a time when the empire was weakening while the papacy, allied with the rising middle class of the Italian cities, whose financial power depended on craftsmanship and the capitalization of land, was also reinforced in Northern Europe by the Benedictine monasteries which had gathered large areas of land into their estates by bequest and by the settling of lordless lands; they had not only been enriched but also invigorated by the great reformers of the monastic life such as St Odo of Cluny (927–42). The humiliation of the Emperor Henry IV at Canossa illustrates this state of affairs. Among European princes the French crown was quickest in profiting by the economic administration. It is therefore the papacy, the monasteries and the new middle class who were now to be the patrons of church builders. In these circumstances European architecture achieved an unprecedented unity and the international style which arose at this time goes by the name of Romanesque.

The Abbey of Cluny in Burgundy, east central France, was at first the great reforming abbey and also one of the most magnificent, and indeed the biggest, building in Europe of its day. This monastic church, the third one on the site, was begun in 1088, three years after the death of

St Gregory VII, the first monk of Cluny to become a pope; the high altar was consecrated in 1095 by Pope Pascal II who had been an Italian monk of the Cluniac reform, and the whole church by Pope Innocent II in 1131. The building fell into disuse and was finally destroyed in the nineteenth century. We know it mostly through restorations. It was a long, barrel-vaulted building with fairly elaborate westwork, double aisles, towers over the crossing and transepts and an elaborate "chevet", a group of chapels off the ambulatory, behind the high altar. This last feature was to become universal in all big medieval European churches. Although Cluny still contained many Italian echoes the short articulation of the many novel parts of the building belonged to a new way of thinking and Cluny had an immediate effect firstly in Burgundy, in such churches as St Marie-Madeleine of Vézelay and at Charité-sur-Loire, and also in Burgundy; its influence was carried to such churches as St Martin of Tours (again in Burgundy) and farther south St Foy at Conques, St Sernin at Toulouse and St James of Compostela. In England, too, a Cluniac trend settled in fairly soon, starting with St Pancras at Lewes (1077) but soon going further afield; abbeys were founded at Castle Acre, Thetford and at Paisley in Scotland (1163) by which time there were nearly forty Cluniac houses in the country.

Besides its great insistence on strict adherence to the rule of St Benedict and on individual spirituality the Cluniac reform also brought with it elaboration of the monastic choral office, a great splendour of vestments and a dramatic emphasis to the liturgy. The allegorical interpretation worked out in Carolingian times by Amalar (c. 815) was further elaborated by a number of theologians such as Yvo of Chartres and Honorius of Autun. The enormously long plan of Cluny and the further removal of the altar from the congregation withdrew the celebrant and his assistant clergy from confronting the congregation and made them into a dramatic spectacle for the congregation to watch, increasingly as a passive audience. The over-elaborate allegorical fantasies of Amalar were applied not only to the liturgy but also to church building. So, for instance, apart from the obvious comparison of the cruciform church plan to the crucified Christ, further analogies on the relationship between different parts of the church and the different parts of the liturgy, as well as parts of the church (that is, gospel side, epistle side) to the wounds of Christ received in the passion, became a matter for repeated speculation.

Astronomical and astrological speculation were also applied to the church building. So, for instance, the medieval conception of the sky as a series of co-axial spheres was referred to the church ceiling and roof, in which the vault was conceived as belonging to the movable stars, whereas the outer timber roof became a fixed firmament. The universal nature of the architecture of this period is obvious in many buildings erected all over Europe during this time, buildings whose superficial differences appear at first to be more striking. As, for example, the strong subdivisions of the church are marked by pointed diaphragm arches which separate huge domes while the walls are subdivided by blind arcades of a kind universal in Europe.

The Byzantine influence on these French buildings is perhaps clearest in the church of St Front at Périgueux whose Greek cross plan appears to be based on the church of the Holy Apostles in Constantinople, as transmitted through St Mark's in Venice. The church of St Nicholas at Bari (1089), in the very south of Italy, displays similar features though here the timber roofed church is subdivided by more diaphragm arches on near-classical piers and columns, an evidence of the romanizing tastes of the

Emperor Frederick II who paid for it. The church of St Miniato al Monte in Florence, begun some thirty years before St Nicholas, is the most faithfully "antique" building of this period in detail, but the whole structure of the building, with its sharp subdivisions, again by diaphragm arches, and its articulation of both outside and interior walls by black and white marble decorations, independent of both the structure and the interior plan of the building, related closely to such contemporary buildings farther north as St Abondio in Como or St Ambrose in Milan, as well as buildings outside Italy, the cathedral at Speyer or the great abbey of Fontrevault (where many Plantagenet British kings are buried), or even the cathedral at Durham, where the detail no longer reflects classical models, and a new energy dictates revolutionary forms.

CHAPTER V

THE AGE OF THE
GREAT CATHEDRALS

Between about 1150 and 1450 European architecture went
through a period of rapid development and of building
activity unprecedented since the fall of the Roman Empire.
While in the preceding period buildings were promoted
by kings and by monastic orders, so that a large proportion of the buildings mentioned were in the country, the
architecture of this period is specifically town architecture.
European trade, so badly wounded by the disruption of
the Mediterranean, was reviving; new centres in the Low
Countries and in Italy had begun to flourish; and half-way,
in Burgundy, an important centre of international trade
was developing. As previously mentioned, the French
monarchs seemed sharply aware of the new situation and
were able to exploit the changes to stabilize the situation
in the country. One of the ablest advisers of the French
crown, Suger, Abbot of St Denis in Paris, was associated
also with the earliest—to our knowledge—fully "pointed"
or "Gothic" building, namely, the abbey over which he
ruled.

St Denis was consecrated in 1140 with much pomp and
remained until the end of the monarchy the burial place
of the kings of France as well as keeper of the essential

coronation regalia. Its greatest treasures were, however, the relics of St Denis, patron of France and allegedly that Athenian convert of St Paul's, who was also the author of a number of mystical works in the neo-Platonic tradition in which a great deal of attention is paid to light as a symbol of divine immanence. It is a doctrine without which stained glass, the most conspicuous and the grandest by-product of this architecture, would be meaningless. The development of stained glass is only one, and not the most important, new element in the situation. There are the riches of the towns, there is the ever increasing splendour of liturgical ceremonial and with it the increasingly fussy allegorical interpretation of both ritual and of the church building. The theatrical atmosphere of Church ceremonial implied an increasing division between the clergy who perform it and the congregation who are gradually reduced to the status of spectators. In many medieval churches this status of theirs was further curtailed: later in the thirteenth century the chancel was enclosed in a screen, sometimes of stone, which admitted only about two or three hundred people into direct participation in the liturgy. The bulk of the congregation then remained outside, but conversely it allowed the nave of larger churches to be used for secular purposes, even sometimes for fairs. The urban church was of tremendous importance as an expression of civic pride and also as a dominating landmark for the countryside around. It also acted as a great stimulus to the economic life of the country.

Conversely, as the liturgy became increasingly remote and popular participation increasingly passive, new forms of devotion developed. The illiterate layman was provided with picture books in which the mysteries of the faith were proposed to his meditation; in the case of rich or powerful patrons these lay devotional books, in the form of illuminated and brightly coloured manuscripts on vellum,

achieved great magnificence. But this devotion also operated at a much deeper level. The greatest of the medieval
mystical teachers, St Bernard of Clairvaux (1090–1153),
sponsored a form of devotion based on personal relationship of the believer to the divine humanity and the extremely powerful Cistercian Order, of which he was the
real leader, carried this kind of devotion through Europe.
The Cistercians were founded in Burgundy, in Cîteaux, in
1098. Their spirit was extremely ascetical and their obser-
vance of the rule of St Benedict literal. They lived in almost
total silence and kept a near-vegetarian diet. Their interest
in farming, together with their determination to found
houses in out of the way, awkward sites (like Waverley
and Riveaulx on the Yorkshire moors) made their coloniz-
ing efforts an extremely powerful influence on the economic
life of Europe. Unlike the Cluniacs, the Cistercians were
not addicted to great display in their churches. The altar
furniture was of iron, the vestments of plain cloth, the
stone left unpainted; but in the cities it was the Cluniac
spirit which prevailed over the Cistercian as far as the
church and its furniture was concerned, even when the
white monks, in the person of Eugenius III (elected 1145),
had risen to the papacy.

Cluny and Cîteaux were separated by only about fifty
miles and the two tendencies which they represented frequently co-existed in the closest proximity. The economic
improvements mentioned earlier suggest the rise not only
in the volume but also in the quality of building activity.
Masonry was becoming highly organized into an international craft and throughout Europe certain well-known
figures were able to find important commissions. As early
as the twelfth century Northern Italian craftsmen from
the Como district (I Cosmati) who were specialists in stone
and mosaic inlays, travelled throughout Europe. The most
famous example of their work in England is the late

thirteenth-century reliquary and sarcophagus of Edward the Confessor behind the high altar of Westminster Abbey.

This placing of the sarcophagus behind the high altar is an innovation to be found all over Europe about this date. The relics of the martyrs enclosed in the catacomb-like crypts under the chancels of Romanesque churches were brought out into the upper church and displayed in a prominent position. With this move the crypt loses some of its original importance; with the relics placed above ground, burial *ad sanctos* is no longer practicable and the devotion for the dead is given another expression in the chantry, the private funerary chapel inside the church building which was to become a disruptive influence on church architecture and a source of abuse later in the thirteenth century; it is not surprising that it is at this time that the magnificent sequence *Dies Irae* appears in the liturgy. The main space of the Gothic church, by the middle of the thirteenth century, was radically different in construction from that of the Romanesque church. With the disappearance of the crypt the building up of the church floor had vanished and the altar which had stood under its baldachino facing the congregation somewhere near the centre of the building was removed to the east end and surrounded, as I said earlier, by a high screen behind which the clerical participants in the liturgical drama could operate undisturbed by the movements in the nave. It is worth noting here perhaps that in Spain, as against the rest of Europe, although the altar was removed to the east in the choir, screens were placed at the west end and this necessitated a long and closed passage to link the western choir and the eastern chancel.

It will be clear from this that the Roman precedent no longer counted for as much in the Gothic church as it had before 1100. The Roman unity of the Western Church was now taken for granted and liturgical practice had become increasingly uniform. It was in the thirteenth century too that two new religious Orders arose, both of them in Italy —the Franciscan (founded in 1209) and the Dominican (founded in *c*. 1220). Both Orders were tied to an urban civilization and both required churches in which the liturgical centre of worship was counter-balanced, if not obscured, by the pulpit. Although the Dominicans followed their own liturgical use, the Franciscans soon became the carriers of liturgical uniformity and it is partly through their activities that the local Roman rite finally became the universal liturgical practice of the Western Church. Architecturally more important, however, was the fact that with the rise of these two Orders the sermon became an increasingly important part of the Christian act of worship and the great vaulted hall-like spaces of these friars' churches are the result of a long development which begins in the Burgundian dominions of France.

This development is the perfection of vaulting. The disadvantages of timber roofs are too obvious to mention; in any case the new vision of the church as a cosmic entity required a more solid enclosure overhead in the church than could be provided by the usual timber roof. Vaulting had, of course, been practised by the Romans, particularly brick and concrete. Concrete, however, was unknown to the medieval builders and stone was the material most readily available to them. It is, therefore, in stone that the first vaults were built. The groined vaulting of antiquity was extremely difficult to carry out in dressed stone. The first successful and individuated school of vaulting developed in Anjou and Poitou under Byzantine influence; the Angevin vaulters adopted a form of dome. Their solution, however, was a clumsy and uneconomic one and it is another form of vaulting, the groined kind, which first appears at Durham cathedral in 1093, which began the prevailing medieval form of roof. The ribbed vault was an enormous technical advance on both the barrel and the groin vault. The barrel vault is a heavy, rigid technical device; the groin vault is extremely awkward to build in stone as it needs an enormous scaffolding on which to rest and has a number of edges which are very difficult to determine geometrically; they could therefore only be built by highly skilled masons using geometrical calculations beyond the means of medieval craftsmen. Ribbed vaults, as the name suggests, carry the weight in thickened edge members: so that only the ribs need to be supported while the building is going up. This kind of vaulting also allows a simplification of the finishing at the crucial joints. The development of the ribbed vault is parallel with the elaboration of medieval wall construction.

Romanesque churches were buildings with solid walls pierced by relatively small windows. Colonnades were either carried on piers or on large solid and simple circular columns. As the blind arcades which decorate so many of the later buildings of that period develop so the great mass of piers of earlier times are split up into a number of components. The church space itself had been broken up into a number of units and this was further emphasized by carrying such column divisions up through the various horizontal divisions of the church so that a number of thicker members were created which, in conjunction with the ribs of the vault, did most of the structural work of the building. Conversely, therefore, walls could be pierced with increasing daring, in spite of the heavy vault, to allow for ever greater areas of stained glass. The most extreme example of this tendency is the Sainte Chapelle in Paris, a shrine which St Louis built in 1243–46 to house the principal relics he had bought from the Byzantines. The ribbed vault and vaulted churches of Northern Europe did, however, present their builders with another problem. The stone vaults, however much they had been lightened by the use of ribs, still presented a great structural problem in terms of sideways thrust. As the church got higher and the vault further from the ground, so this thrust of the stone mass of the vault outwards became a more important factor in the building. Medieval masons were not equipped to deal with this matter by calculation and had to rely on experiment. There are records of many structural failures —a dramatic one is the fall of the timber spire of Beauvais cathedral about twenty years after its construction, and a glaring one the collapse of the nave of Utrecht cathedral in a seventeenth-century hurricane which left the choir standing. In the early Romanesque churches the problem did not really appear.

Vaults were an exception and the walls in any case remarkably thick, enough to carry the clumsiest vault safely. It is only late in the eleventh century that attempts to overcome the difficulties presented by a vault supported on a pierced wall were made. The piercing of the walls to allow sufficient light into the building and make it a unified volume accentuated the structural problems: the development of the vault and the enlargement of the glass window area worked together. The plans of many succeeding cathedrals demonstrated clearly the expedient used. If you look at any such engraved plan you will find the thin lines of the windows and the criss-cross phalanx of the vault; also you will notice the heavier accents at right angles to the axis of the building. These will be the columns on the inside and the buttresses on the outside of the building. The sideways thrust of the tall principal vault of the building was taken up by the vaults of the lower aisles leaving an open clerestory rising over the arcades between the nave and aisle. Frequently an intermediate gallery, called the triforium, also appears between clerestory and colonnade, but it is not a universal feature.

The buttresses at first take the shape of simple cross

walls of stone, or even just a thickening of the walls. But
within a hundred years of the first ribbed vault at Durham
cathedral the buttresses are moved outside the main structure of the building beyond the aisle and a breach of stone
is built between the nave piers which support the main
weight of the vault and the buttress; frequently, too, a
pinnacle is placed on top of the buttress to anchor the
weight more securely to the ground. This kind of structural feature, which appears in France well before 1200
(Chartres, Bourges) is introduced in England a few
decades later and made much of in Germany in even later
years. The relationship of pinnacle to buttress is of particular interest since in 1453 a German master mason,
Mathew Roriczer, set down a geometrical method used
by masons in relating the proportions of the pinnacle to
the buttress by drawing a square round a whole buttress,
inscribing another square at 45° inside it, and a third
square parallel to the first one inside the second one. This
simple geometrical device was much favoured by many
masons; it resulted in a series of dimensions related as
$1 : \sqrt{2}$; from Roriczer as well as from other documents
we know that besides this another system of proportion
much favoured during the Middle Ages was based on the
equilateral triangle which allowed the mason to operate
with the system proportions based on the ratio $2 : 3$. It is
important to remember that in the Middle Ages, as in
earlier times, the decimal system did not operate nor were
arabic numerals familiar. The mason therefore found it
extremely difficult to work by calculation and relied, in
most cases, on the much simpler geometrical procedure.
The simple geometrical figures not only served the designer
to establish a coherent system of proportion but such was
their trust in the inner harmony of the world fabric that
many of them believed that geometrical harmony helped
in some degree to assure structural stability.

These beliefs were elaborated with the increasing size of church buildings (in height more than in area) as the fourteenth century succeeded the thirteenth; and with the multiplying of ever more far-fetched and elaborate commentaries on the liturgy and on church building, of which the best known perhaps is that of William Durandus (1230–96). Durandus concerned himself with all particulars: the priests' vesting, the colour of each vestment, the details of the Mass, the ornaments and the building itself. His authority was very great and the order of bishops' offices which he compiled became one of the sources of the *Pontificale Romanum*. Like Durandus' Pontifical the various features of Gothic architecture such as the pointed arch, the groined vault and the flying buttress, soon became universal. The architecture of the Cistercian monks, for instance, is easily recognized. It is they who carried the groined vault with them and to them too go the colonnaded apse with an ambulatory behind, off which a series of small chapels opens. In England, in particular, the Gothic fashion took very quickly; the groined vault, as mentioned before, had appeared at Durham (1093) and less than a century later the French master mason, William of Sens, rebuilt Canterbury cathedral in the new manner; the authority of the primatial see of England established this kind of architecture securely upon English soil. Soon many other cathedrals followed suit, the most splendid one perhaps at Lincoln, and a little later at Salisbury and Peterborough. In 1245 Henry III ordered the rebuilding of Westminster Abbey under the supervision of a master mason who may well have been a Frenchman. Germany, of course, is not divided from France as England is and the influences permeated across the Rhine as they did across the channel. The Cistercians worked their way into Germany as much as into France but Angevin builders, modelling themselves on such a building as Poitiers cathedral, also found work in Germany, as for example at the cathedral at Munster; perhaps it is the Angevin churches which are ancestor of the typical German hall church.

The hall church, whose nave and aisles are almost at the same level, became very popular both in Germany and Italy. Obvious early examples are the church of St Elizabeth at Marburg and St Severus at Erfurt, while in Italy the church of Santa Maria Novella in Florence, and even the upper church of St Francis in Assisi, have a certain amount in common with them. The Cistercians had the same effect in Italy on a minor scale as elsewhere, but the powerful influence during the thirteenth century in both the Rhineland and Italy were the two great preaching Orders, the Dominicans and the Franciscans. The elaborate allegories of Durandus and the great machinery of liturgical and quasi-liturgical symbolism broke up when it came to the hall church. The primary requirement was extensive preaching space with ancillary space for the procession. In the hall church the liturgy is pushed firmly to the east end; a simplified space is no longer worked out to carry the elaborate encyclopedic symbolic message of the great cathedrals. While the hall churches became broader and lighter the cathedrals in their turn went ever higher, in particular the great churches of the rich cities: Beauvais, Cologne, Lübeck, Barcelona, rose to enormous heights. Beauvais cathedral typifies the ambitious spirit of the burghers. It is the tallest medieval church in the world, 158 feet high, but only the chancel was finished and the building remained unbuilt, with a tiny Romanesque nave and a huge, overwhelming chancel and transept.

Both money and piety seemed to have run out. The grandiloquent simplicities of thirteenth-century architecture were over-ambitious and by 1300 a new mood of uncertainty appeared in Europe. The papacy throughout the fourteenth century lost its hold in Rome. In 1309 the popes moved to Avignon and after their return to Rome anti-popes remained there until 1408. Sectaries were beginning to threaten the central unity of Catholic Christendom and Christian princes, seeing the weakening of papal authority, made capital of the situation and indeed traded their support of this or that pope in return for concessions. The religious dissensions, such as that caused by the Albigen-sian heresy in the south of France in the reign of St Louis, was succeeded by armed religious conflict between the Catholic Christians all recognizing the central authority of the Roman Pontiff but giving their support to alterna-tive occupiers of the papal throne. It is in this atmosphere that medieval architecture is transformed into something less overwhelmingly assured, more fragmentary, more in-volved, more warped. The late medieval architects, those who in France are called flamboyant and in England per-pendicular, belonged to an international movement whose principal monuments are the cathedrals of Prague, Stras-bourg and Vienna and the choir of Gloucester. Not only was the fabric of Christendom weakened by the machina-tions around the papacy but all Christian worship appears to have undergone a very radical modification. The ten-dency, which had already been noticeable early in the Middle Ages, for the Mass to become a splendid spectacle performed before a group of clergy enclosed inside a choir within the huge cathedral, and invisible to the people, naturally affected individual worship. Lay attendance at the liturgy ceased to be a communal act and became an atrophied form of service by the eleventh century.

The custom had gradually arisen also for every priest not only to attend but to celebrate the liturgy daily. The pro-liferation of altars which had begun in Ottonian times now assumed vast proportions, large churches were crowded not only with small chapels but also with chantries, small private burial enclosures inside the body of the church, each one with its altar at which a privately employed priest could celebrate Mass. The congregation, therefore, had also altered radically. Those attending the liturgy no longer participated vocally but quite often limited themselves to attendance at some private Mass or to attending only at the moment of consecration. Communion of those present ceased to be a normal part of liturgical participation. Mass attendance, in fact, was reduced to the absurd when holes were pierced in the wall for people in the churchyard to be able to see the host and chalice when the priest raised them at the elevation. This fragmentation of piety is mirrored by the increasingly particularized and intensified expression of feeling in the painting and sculpture of that period. The preoccupation with private piety and Masses for the dead was heightened in the middle of the fourteenth century by a series of particularly virulent and deathly plagues which are known to us as the Black Death; they depleted the population of Europe and had a disastrous, if temporary, effect on economic life, and put a brake on building for some years.

It is not surprising that the work of the second half of the century was more tortuous and more elaborate than what had gone before. The desire to raise a heavy stone vault enormously high, the desire which produced Beauvais, no longer operated. The vault was now brought lower down but curious new effects were sought for. Sometimes vaulting ribs were no longer separated from the supporting piers by capitals but the mouldings were made continuous with the columns; the ribs were not used to divide the vault into four or six obvious planes but were now drawn into elaborate and sometimes quite arbitrary patterns. In England a system of vaulting, called fan-vaulting, was developed in which the vaults appeared as cones warped outwards from the shaft of the column; they were usually covered by a tracery of thin, non-structural ribs. The most famous instances are the Cardinal's gateway at Christchurch and the chapel of King's College, Cambridge; a more complicated form appears in the roof of Christ Church, Oxford, and in the chapel of Henry VII in Westminster Abbey. This last example was built between 1500 and 1520 and is a brilliantly accomplished building in the medieval tradition though already, even here, an alien mode is introduced—the king's tomb and the altar are the work of an Italian craftsman imported from Renaissance Italy.

The second part of the Middle Ages is very much the time of cathedral building and I have tended to emphasize the cathedrals in discussing medieval architecture since it is obvious that the brilliant and original master masons would be employed in cathedrals rather than in humble parish churches. It is, however, also the period in which, all over Europe, a parish organization was consolidated and during which innumerable parish churches were built; churches which, as I pointed out in the previous chapter, had become the archetype of the Christian church. Many of the cathedrals were built in the course of one, or very few, building campaigns. A campaign like that might last fifteen or twenty years and would mobilize the resources of the district to a considerable extent. It would also follow the design of one master or of a definite group who might be local masons but might also be famous international figures, summoned expressly for this particular job. In the case of a parish church local talent was more likely to be used than foreign craftsmanship and the fashion set for the nearest cathedral or monastery might have an enormous effect on the course of local building. It is almost impossible to generalize about the Western parish church. Plans varied enormously not only from district to district but also from decade to decade; money was not always available in such bulk as it had been for cathedral building so that the parish church might take shape over a period of several centuries. Plans were much more varied than in the Byzantine world and buildings ranged from quasi-cathedrals such as St Sebald's at Nuremberg or Boston parish church, to very humble churches composed of a single hall with an open timber roof: there are many of these all over Europe.

The steady stream of Gothic parish church building went on long after a new revolution had taken place in European art. This revolution had started in Italy where conflicting city states varied their allegiance from emperor to pope, from the King of Spain to the King of France—or even between rival popes; and this disastrous situation stimulated a new political attitude which found its expression in an architecture based on antique models. This was to dominate Europe for the next four hundred years.

CHAPTER VI

HUMANISM AND

PATRISTICS

Throughout the fourteenth century at the papal court in Avignon and at some French universities there was great interest in the study of ancient texts. Meanwhile in Italy the towns had risen to great power and prosperity and were beginning to assert a new independence both from the papacy and from the empire. This assertion of independence is what we call the Renaissance. It found its expression, as far as the arts are concerned, in the adoption of the outward forms of Roman antiquity as a token of the desire to return to ancient grandeur and virtue. In Rome this was developed in the direction of a return to the style of the Emperor Constantine, the first great church builder, and of the restoration of the primitive authority of the Roman Church. For the reformers of government in republican cities like Florence it meant an appeal to the democratic virtues of those early days of the Roman Republic, of which such historians as Livy wrote. To certain autocratic princes, such as Sforza in Milan or Malatesta of Rimini, it meant the emulation of Roman splendour in imperial times, while to those princes who in the next century tried to establish their independence from Rome the use of ancient motifs implied an independence of their natural authority from the dictates of the Church.

The appeal of antiquity was not a new one: throughout the Middle Ages people were interested in the way the ancients had designed and built, but thought of classical architecture as existing in myth. However, as I mentioned in the last chapter, they became increasingly independent of their direct influence. In the fifteenth century a great enthusiasm for ancient literature moved many scholars; much learning and energy were expended on producing correct texts of ancient writers by comparing and correct- ing old available manuscripts. The same method was, of course, applied to the writings of the early Fathers. Not unnaturally certain artists applied scholarly methods to ancient monuments instead of texts. At the beginning of the fifteenth century two Florentine sculptors, Brunelleschi (1377–1446) and Donatello (1386/7–1466) travelled down to Rome and measured and recorded several Roman build- ings. The first product of this trip was a chantry chapel which Brunelleschi designed for the Pazzi family just out- side the walls of the Franciscan church of the Holy Cross in Florence; a small building which showed correct classi- cal detail but which turned out to be more like a Byzantine chapel than a Western medieval one. It was a square build- ing on the plan, with an open porch in front, the nave broader than it was long covered by a square dome on a drum, also a large square apse covered by a saucer dome in which the altar stood detached from the walls. This kind of plan indicated a new attitude to the design of a church building.

The small dome of the Pazzi chapel was soon to be dwarfed by the huge and most important dome which Brunelleschi raised over the centre of Florence cathedral some years later. This was not a circular dome over a square space but an octagonal dome over the octagonal crossing and it retained something of earlier medieval characteristics. This dome represented a great technical achievement and the economy of Brunelleschi's solution of the structural problem enabled many other architects to use a form of dome construction.

It is worth noting that what may look medieval to us was thought at the time to have an antique character. In the fifteenth and sixteenth centuries people did not have a clearly defined idea of what ancient buildings looked like and quite often mistook medieval classicizing in building for ancient ones, so for instance the baptistery of Florence cathedral was thought to be the ancient Roman Temple of Mars which was mentioned in historical texts. In the same way, most of the manuscript sources used by the humanists in search of authentic texts dated back not to antiquity— as Renaissance scholars thought—but were products of the Carolingian classic revival. In fact, the characteristic humanist handwriting, on which the letter forms of modern printing are based, was originally a fifteenth-century revival of a ninth-century script. In the fifteenth century Italy was undoubtedly the most important country in Europe, not only spiritually and artistically, but also economically; what the Italians did had therefore very strong repercussions on the rest of Europe. The papacy indeed was not quite as firmly lodged in Rome as we think it was. There had been the schisms in the Avignon exile and the papal court quite often resided in other French and Italian cities; and although the schisms were closed with the election of Martin V at Pisa in 1415 the pope remained free to travel not only in the patrimony of Peter but throughout Europe; he did in fact frequently stay outside Rome for fairly lengthy periods. Eugenius IV spent several seasons in Florence during the Ecumenical Council there (1438–45). Rome was not the place where the first innovations took place; but rather the great republican cities such as

Florence and Venice. Venice made the greater contribution in painting. Florentine innovators were painters, sculptors and architects in equal measure. The three who made the more radical Florentine revolution originally were Brunelleschi for architecture, Donatello for sculpture— whom I mentioned as having travelled to Rome together— and Masaccio for painting. Architectural handbooks tend to speak of the Renaissance church as being centralized or even as man-centred. Brunelleschi himself was very interested in the centralized plan as is obvious from the Pazzi chapel, but his most famous two buildings besides the dome of Florence cathedral, are two cruciform basilicas, the churches of San Lorenzo and of Santo Spirito. The innovations which these two buildings showed are not so much a metaphysical man-centredness but rather a new respect for the main altar and a much stronger emphasis on the importance of the chancel. They are quite different from the huge friars' preaching halls of the century before: they are ordered and elaborately articulated structures whose effect is made by clear distinction between the skeleton of the building (that is, the columns and piers which perform the main structural work) and its tissue, the walls. The architects of the fifteenth century, Brunelleschi himself and his later contemporaries, Alberti, San Gallo and the great masters of the following century, Raphael, Michelangelo and Palladio, continued to play on this contrast: many of their churches obtain their effect through this contrast between the dark stone structure and the cool white walls. The skeleton emphasizes yet inevitably reduces the importance of fresco painting. The canvas or panel in an architectural frame became increasingly individuated and independent of the wall surface.

The revolution of church architecture is quite obvious when one considers how fifteenth-century architects treated the church façade. They were not satisfied to follow medieval precedent, which they considered corrupt, but they could not appeal to an early Christian precedent which would have the then necessary force of the antique. They had therefore to endow the classical detail which they wished to remould with a Christian meaning of their own. The first essay in that direction was Alberti's church of St Sigismund (the Tempio Malatestiano in Rimini) where the principal façade is a triple arcade; the central arch is pierced by a door, the two side ones carry the tomb of Sigismund and his consort. It will be recalled that Roman temples did not have solid walls like the churches of the fifteenth century but were surrounded by open arcades much like those of the Greeks. Roman temples could therefore provide no precedent for Renaissance architects and the façade of Sigismund is not modelled on a temple but on a Roman triumphal arch. There was a famous arch in Rimini only about twenty minutes' walk away from the church so that the most casual observer must have caught the reference. The entrance was analogous to the two tombs and implied that Sigismund and his consort Isotta had triumphed over death; so the church-goer was entering into glory by passing through the church door.

Alberti was responsible for several other church façades and he speculated much on the problem provided by the typical basilican plan current in Italy then of a tall nave with lower aisles, which worried many architects for such a long time. On the whole the earlier Renaissance architects accepted the discrepancy and, like Alberti, linked the two lines by swages. In the middle of the fifteenth century the great Venetian architect, Palladio, made the innovation of treating the nave as though it were a separate church with a triangular pediment and the whole church of nave and aisles as if it were another separate unit: so that the church had one narrow triangular roof line over the nave

and a wider and lower roof line projecting out of it on both
sides and covering the aisles. Quite often, too, the central
portion of the building was given columns of higher relief,
while the aisles only had flat pilasters, so that the two
separate units were visibly distinguished. Palladio grafted
this solution on to Alberti's original triumphal arch
scheme; after 1600 it became a standard way of treating
a church façade throughout Europe. The solution of the
formal problems cannot hide the fact that in the fifteenth
and sixteenth centuries there was a conflict about church
building, a conflict which is quite often described as one
between the clergy and the artists (although the issue was
not quite as simple as that) which is a renewal of the old
polarity between martyrium and basilica, between the centralized and the long axial form of building. This conflict
is best illustrated by the lengthy and confused history of the
building of St Peter's church in Rome.

The original basilica was placed over the tomb of St
Peter by the Emperor Constantine in A.D. 345, and was a
great five-aisled church with a narthex, to which various

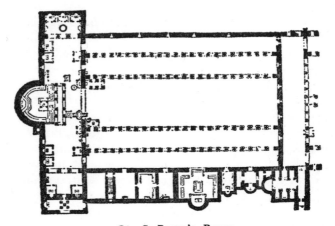

OLD ST PETER'S, ROME

alterations were made in the course of its millennian existence. By the time of Nicholas V (1447–55) the building had become so decayed that piecemeal repair could no longer save it and a completely new structure was required. At the same time, since St Peter's was one of the most venerable churches in the whole of Christendom, any radical alterations in the layout and conception of the building were considered with great hesitation by the more conservative members of the papal court, and even by Pope Nicholas and his successors. Nevertheless, Julius II, who was elected in 1503, early in his reign appointed Donato Bramante architect of the building; he began to work out a huge centralized church on the scale of some of the larger antique buildings whose ruins were to be seen in Rome. It seems clear both from the character of the drawings and from the foundation medal struck in 1506, that this initial plan was for a great cross-in-square, with the ends of the cross projecting beyond the enclosing square wall as apses, and a system of minor domes and

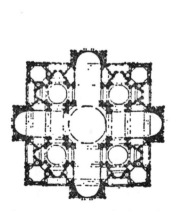
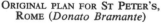
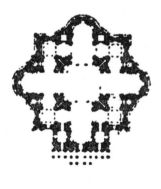

ORIGINAL PLAN FOR ST PETER'S,   PROJECT FOR ST PETER'S,
ROME (*Donato Bramante*)   ROME (*Michelangelo*)

spires in the corners and a huge semi-circular dome carried on a drum of columns over the central space. Under this great dome was to stand the high altar sited over the tomb of St Peter.

This dome was a building problem beyond the experience of Bramante, as it was beyond the experience of most of his contemporaries, and the scheme was in fact never completely clarified. When Bramante died only the foundations of the piers and of the walls had been laid. He was succeeded as architect of the building by his nephew, the great painter Raphael, who revised the scheme to make the church into the more usual longitudinal shape; and although he accepted the basic modulation of the building he nevertheless understood that the piers designed by his uncle were inadequate to carry the great weight of the dome. The dome remained a constituent part of the conception of St Peter's and all subsequent designs took account of the weakness of Bramante's piers and made various attempts to strengthen them without essentially damaging the plan which he left behind. In Raphael's day the perfection of the plan was marred when a longitudinal layout was imposed by ecclesiastical advisers. Raphael's successor, Baldassare Peruzzi, who may also have been a pupil of Bramante, again modified the plans; in 1527, however, the Emperor Charles V sacked Rome and the economic disasters which followed stopped any work on St Peter's for many years. Then another minor architect, Antonio de Sangallo, redesigned the building in a somewhat different spirit. He had more success than his predecessors. He had actually managed to enlarge the piers which would probably have supported the dome he designed, a two-storied one, adequately. What is more, Sangallo modified the plan very considerably in a way which may even have been suggested by some later project of Bramante. While he kept the plan of the main building nearly central, a semi-detached secondary building, carrying two spires, not unlike some Carolingian westworks, was placed at the west end. This compromise project may even have developed from certain ideas of Bramante's.

It is perhaps worth remembering that half-way in time between the laying of the foundation stone and Sangallo's appointment, Martin Luther had been excommunicated in Germany and that his excommunication was indirectly tied to the building of St Peter's; it was the sale of indulgences to swell the building funds of St Peter's that had originally provoked his anger. Finally, about 1537, Michelangelo, who was perhaps the greatest artist of his age and other ones as well, was put in charge of the building. Michelangelo abandoned Sangallo's compromise scheme and based himself on Bramante's centralized project. Again his was a cross-in-square building with smaller domes at the corners and a big dome on a drum at the centre; but the piers supporting the dome were now made very massive and the breakdown of the volume, the modulation of the building, was much more violent and abrupt than Bramante's rather gentle, if complicated, scheme. Moreover, Michelangelo's scheme contained an ambiguity; it was not wholly centralized about two apses. His church had three apses but at the west end there was a huge open portico which rose to the whole height of the building. When Michelangelo died in 1564 he was nearly ninety and his building was far from finished; the central piers had been carried as far as the drum.

After Michelangelo's death many small modifications were made to his scheme, though the central idea remained intact until 1602, when a decision was reached to extend the church westwards and to abandon the huge portico— a decision which went back to the proceedings of the Council of Trent in Michelangelo's lifetime. Although the solution was carried out in terms of the same scale as

Michelangelo's, the grandeur of his conception was severely damaged and the dome, which in his project dominated the square in front of the church, was masked along the approach by the bulk of the building. It was not until many years later (in 1666) that St Peter's was given those impressive colonnades by another great architect, Gian Lorenzo Bernini, colonnades which complete our picture of the church.

Bernini was also responsible for two other important features which attract the visitor's attention as he enters the building. One is the high altar placed where both Bramante and Michelangelo wanted it, directly under the dome, and supported on four spiral columns (whose design is based on the supposed order of the columns in the temple in Jerusalem, one of which had been brought as a relic to Rome in the Middle Ages), the other is the altar of the throne which occupies the east end of the church. This, like the canopy of the high altar, is of bronze, partly gilt. It is, in fact, a large reliquary containing the chair which St Peter is supposed to have used for his throne as bishop of Rome, but the actual relic is not visible to the spectator and is completely concealed in an elaborate bronze confection. Above the container, which is held up by great bronze statues of the four doctors of the church, is a window glazed with amber glass; at the centre of it appears the vision of the Holy Ghost; and the oval painting is surrounded by gold rays, radiating in all directions. When the sun is shining, therefore, this window appears to be a natural source of light and the spiritual illumination seems to shine down directly on the throne of Peter. This whole construction is about seventy feet high and forms an elaborate allegorical fantasy, a kind of theological background to papal ceremonial.

Bernini's bronze pageantries would have been totally alien to the earlier artists who had worked on St Peter's.

Michelangelo would have despised any appeal to the spectator through theatrical illusion. But then the artists who lived at the beginning of the sixteenth century were the last Christian artists who could take their faith for granted and thought of themselves as working in a Christian Europe which, however else it was divided, was at any rate all one within the body of the Church. Their fascination with the theme of the centralized church, a theme which was used to exalt the idea of God's perfection as mirrored by the perfect organization of the totally symmetric building, was the last grand self-contained statement of an overwhelming theological theme in visual terms.

Michelangelo and his contemporaries, and even more the artists of the two generations before them, had a close acquaintance with the liturgy in which a new interest developed as a result of the discovery of certain patristic writings. Certain of their contemporaries, such as St Antoninus, archbishop of Florence, were also concerned anew with the liturgy as a pastoral activity. Fifteenth-century church builders showed the high altar as the focal point of their churches and attributed a new importance to the liturgical action as a community function. Alberti, for instance, the first architect since ancient times to write a treatise on his profession, was himself a priest and made it clear in his writings that his church buildings were not only conceived as carrying certain abstract symbols but also that they were intended to embody ideas on liturgical reform and liturgical propriety; he was determined to give proper importance to the high altar of the church, to reshape the ornaments according to his idea of the usage of the early church and free it from medieval accretions. The tone of his writings is very reminiscent of some of the leaders of the liturgical reform movement in the late nineteenth century who were as determined to remove seventeenth- and eighteenth-century accretions from their churches as Alberti was concerned to remove medieval ones. But the artists of Michelangelo's generation and their successors lost the Renaissance certainties. Europe was no longer the undivided Christian world but was sharply cleft into a Protestant and a Catholic part; while the Protestants and their sympathizers tended to emphasize all the Puritan aspects of the Christian religion, to eschew effect and even despise visual pleasure, Catholic worship moved from former certainty to doubt and unease which was, when expressed by masters like Michelangelo, perhaps even more touching and splendid than the former generation. In fact, after the shock of the division which showed itself in the uncertainties of late sixteenth-century architecture, a regrouping of forces took place in the seventeenth century; a regrouping which brought with it a shift of emphasis. Certainties were no longer being displayed by heraldic devices, they were now being avidly claimed.

Until the sixteenth century religious buildings had been, for most civilizations, the important and dominant buildings of any city. At certain times all valuable architectural experiment that was going on was part of church building programmes. The term "medieval architecture" recalls instantly the vaulting appropriate to a medieval church rather than that of any castle or palace. Baroque architecture, however, suggests as much, if not more, one of the great princely palaces such as Versailles, rather than any particular church. The fragmentation of European religious unity had transformed the earlier political conflict into religious wars; difference in religious opinion did not coincide with international boundaries: and so the doctrine of *cuius regio eius religio* was formed with the implication that the king provided a norm of religious opinion for his subjects. This by-product of the Reformation would certainly not have been acceptable to the great early reformers like Luther or Calvin. From the Catholic point of view it eroded the position of the Holy See in European politics, as well as finances, and made the Papal States into a minor factor in the conflicts among the growing European states. This meant that the long fight which had been waged by certain theologians against the excessive political claims of the papacy had not only been won but that the pendulum had swung too far to the other way and political authority was now claiming excessive jurisdiction in spiritual matters.

This development is clearly reflected in church architecture, in particular where the church has no connection with a palace or some seat of authority. In the early church the bishop, with his clergy around him, sat on the east side of the altar while the congregation faced him from the other side; in the Middle Ages his position moved to the epistle side of the chancel as the altar was moved even further east; but a bishop was still the dominant figure at any liturgical celebration. There had, it is true, been an episode at the time of the Frankish Empire when the sacred imperial throne had assumed a special position in the church building. On the whole, however, the king and emperor did not have any more than an ornate stall to mark their place in the church, at any rate in Western Europe; not, that is, until the seventeenth century when, as in the late Middle Ages, the altar is again incorporated into a huge construction which in its turn is dominated by a large, illusionistic altar piece or sculpture (of which the altar chair in St Peter's is an outstanding example) while the seat of the monarch assumes the appearance of a theatrical box.

The isolation of the monarch typified the general isolation of the worshippers with respect to the congregation in the Baroque church. The member of the congregation was no more an actor in the public act of worship than the medieval Christian peeping through a spy hole at the elevation of the Host as he stood in the churchyard. This is made clear not only from the turn church building took about this time but also from the development of church music and devotional literature. From the sixteenth century onwards church music becomes increasingly elaborate and no composer of any stature, from then until the eighteenth century, composes Masses for congregational use. The vast quantity of liturgical music is intended for professional performance; in the seventeenth century Masses began to include elaborate solo parts. In the same way, devotional literature of private prayers for use during liturgical celebrations developed all over Europe. In some countries, particularly in Eastern Germany and the Slavonic Catholic countries, this development is marked by a procedure borrowed from the Protestants: while the clergy celebrate the Eucharist in the chancel the congregation sings hymns in the nave without reference to the doings of the clergy. Whichever way it is considered, in the Baroque and Rococo periods the liturgy is no longer seen as a public act of worship in the Christian community but more as a devotional exercise performed by the priest and his assistants before an audience of passive spectators, whose piety is expressed entirely by its private devotions.

The division of the worshipping body into audience and actors is further emphasized by the spectacular and theatrical development of church building in the second half of the eighteenth century. The altar, which had of course been pushed right to the back of the church in the Middle Ages, now becomes part of an elaborate sculptural group involving altar and reredos, while much invention is devoted to finding new ways of using light to dramatize the already theatrical east end. The golden flow from the window above the altar of the chair in St Peter's, mentioned earlier, is one of the earliest instances of such dramatic illusionism. This effect is taken up particularly by Spanish and German architects; lighting, in fact, was no longer used as an accidental element in some elaborate allegory, but became the general means of inducing dramatic effect through highlighting the already tortured compositions. Moreover, this was no longer applied to the east end alone: the space of the whole church was laid out before the spectator. The plans were based on elaborate schemes composed of intersecting ellipses which were reflected by the vaulted ceilings so that the entering worshipper found himself in a progression of half-defined curvilinear chambers, often lit at different intensities; sometimes the body of the church was relatively dim and worked up to a culmination in the harsh and dramatic light of the theatrical chancel. Such contrasts were particularly spectacular in Spain. In Germany the tendency was to allow sufficient light into the church for the volume of the building to be quite visible; but most elaborate visual games were played by painting the ceilings with a dissolving panorama of some historical event, developing over gently undulating cupolas whose complex outlines the spectator could not unravel. All over the Austrian Empire and Southern Germany such churches appeared in large quantities in the first half of the eighteenth century.

It was a time when the Turkish menace had at long last been dealt with and the religious and dynastic wars of the previous century succeeded by a period of relative calm. In the building boom which succeeded the earlier privations, a period of war and austerity, the prince abbots and prince bishops of the prosperous German-speaking empire found this theatricality a useful condiment to the large bland spaces of their builders and a spice for the passive piety of their flocks. But the pride and spectacle were not all that exclusive. The glittering Rococo church of intricate outline and painted promise was the vision of paradise which even the Bavarian peasant could appreciate.

The missionaries who left Europe to carry the Catholic faith to the Far East and to the New World were mostly Italian and Spanish—certainly the bulk were of Latin origin. Inevitably they took with them the architectural ideas of the community into which they were born. It is worth remembering here, that the classicism which provided the framework in which all architectural ideas at the time operated was not considered to be a historical style as we might think of it, but rather a timeless and absolute point of reference by which all architecture could be judged. This conception of classicism was so prevalent that various attempts were made during the period of counter reform to divorce it from pagan precedent, either by appealing to the "natural law of beauty" or by suggesting that it was a direct product of divine revelation. The Spanish Jesuit Villapanda, for instance, suggested in the year 1600 that the orders of architecture were first used by King Solomon in the Jerusalem temple, as a result of direct inspiration, and that their divine origin made them the essential ornament of all Christian buildings.

Such ideas were reflected by the work of church builders in New England and Canada; John Wood of Bath (who had such a strong influence on English architecture) was a firm follower of Villapanda and believed that at Bath he was constructing a miniature of the new Jerusalem. Those in America set out to meet more or less stone-age civilizations; they accompanied armies which were in any case determined to destroy these near-savage societies. The missionaries, however, who travelled to China and India encountered mature and sophisticated civilizations. Such rulers as Akbar the Great in India toyed with Christianity, were permissive towards missionaries and occasionally employed Christian artists. The Jesuits who went to India and on to China provide the first full-scale attempt in modern times of conversion by example and silent witness. In China, in particular, the Jesuit missionaries were determined to learn Chinese ways and absorb Chinese civilization. Some of them, in spite of being foreigners, became Mandarins, that is Chinese civil servants, by passing an examination of an extremely stringent kind; and although their building activities were relatively insignificant at least one of them, the Italian painter Giuseppe Castiglioni, became one of the minor masters of Chinese painting in the sixteenth century.

Such an attitude of passive witness would have been unthinkable for Europeans in Central or South America either spiritually, politically or artistically. European travellers may have been awed by the size of the buildings they found there but they were also appalled by the harshness and satanic cruelty of the decoration. Missionaries imported European books wholesale to provide examples for the local craftsmen on whom they relied and it is the interpretation of these craftsmen, who quite often had never seen European block building, that gives European Baroque its American flavour when it appears on the other side of the Atlantic. The volume of building, however, was not very large and very few outstanding figures appear. The pilgrimage churches of the Good Jesus at Braga and Corigonhas at Campo, in Brazil, are the work of the crippled sculptor Aleijadinho and are among the most remarkable masterpieces of Baroque architecture anywhere

CHAPTER VII

RETREAT AND REVIVAL

The French Revolution of 1789 marked a point of no return in the development of the Church. As a result of this upheaval France became a secular State for the first time in her history. The respective autonomy of Church and State finally replaced the idea of *cuius regio eius religio* as a standard of relationship between Church and State, a standard which many other European and American countries were soon to emulate. Not that this was an entirely new condition. About the time of the French Revolution a liberal Catholic State, Poland, was partitioned by Protestant Prussia, Catholic Austria and Orthodox Russia, and this partition demonstrated the complete irrelevance of religious loyalties in political affairs.

The separation between Church and State achieved by the French Revolution was not immediate; Napoleon both abused and deferred to papal authority. The restored monarchy made a gesture towards the pre-revolutionary conditions. Nevertheless, throughout the Western world since the eighteenth century, the State was increasingly conceived as an independent institution to be obeyed through its own "natural" laws and human society as being bound to its rulers by a social and not a divine contract. Authority, therefore, did not need religious sanction for the exercise of authority, or solemn forms of public worship to express this sanction.

So church building was placed in a new context. It was no longer the plain duty of the state and government to provide and maintain grandiose places of worship. And this change in context came about at a time when the whole nature of architecture was undergoing a revolution started off by violent and unmanageable forces.

This last revolution began modestly enough when, in the middle of the eighteenth century, familiarity with non-European cultures became sufficiently common for scholars to question the exclusive and extra-historical authority of the antique classical orders. At the same time the architecture of antiquity was re-examined with a new, irreverent eye. The Greek mainland, which had been in Turkish hands since the fourteenth century, became fairly easily accessible to European architects since the Turks wanted at long last to live in peace with the Infidels; as a result of this the old global view of classical antiquity became fragmented and the distinction between Greek and Roman architecture again undermined the authority of the classics. So it happened that French revolutionaries and many other sympathizers saw a newly revived "primitive" Greek architecture as contributing to the idealizing of republican virtue while others, certain Italian architects in particular, clung to antiquity as providing a standard of absolute aesthetic rightness. As against these two approaches yet a third attitude was more popular: one which regarded the vocabulary of classical forms as just another way of decking out buildings which might alternatively be given Gothic, Turkish, Indian or Chinese ornament, depending on the place for which they were designed or the associations which they were to invoke.

There had, in the eighteenth century, been a revival of interest in medieval architecture, promoted by antiquarians, a revival which was allied to the desire of the newly enfranchized higher middle classes in Western Europe to achieve a more liberal *milieu* than had been demanded by the established aristocracy for its more formal proceedings. The medieval airs which certain oligarchs gave themselves also became an adjunct to the pretences of nobility in which so many of them indulged.

By the break of the century the Gothic revival had gathered strength and changed its nature. It had become allied with the Romantic Movement and had been given somewhat contradictory political and social undertones. In Continental Europe it had become associated with legitimism, that is, the movement which wanted to re-establish government through the hereditary principle. In England it had—particularly through the writings of Augustus Welby Pugin—become associated with social protest. To Pugin, medieval architecture was the expression of an integrated society where the dignity of the person was safeguarded by religious sanctions, where labour was freely offered and remunerated and where the blight of the industrial revolution did not affect human environment and the social fabric. Pugin urged a return to Catholic faith and Gothic architecture; in principle, the Gothic architecture of the late fifteenth century, which he thought to have been the last valid expression of Catholic society before the reformation. This return, he thought, would put Western society back on the right road of development. As his prescription was not seriously tested we shall never know how correct it was. At any rate, his writings prompted a revival of medievalized building in this country, in Germany and ultimately in France. Moreover, his devotion to Gothic architecture impelled a number of influential architects, such as Giles Gilbert Scott in this country and Viollet-le-Duc in France, to strip any post-medieval accretions from medieval churches and even to restore existing medieval buildings to the best kind of Gothic which the restorer may have thought suitable. Many beautiful churches were destroyed through this kind of enthusiasm; but Pugin's influence on building proper was perhaps more important. His best known executed work is the Gothic fancy-dress which he designed for Sir Charles Barry's Houses of Parliament; independently he was also a very prolific builder and designed the new Catholic cathedrals in Birmingham and Newcastle, as well as working on many monastic and other religious buildings up and down Britain.

The great aesthete and critic, John Ruskin, translated Pugin's influence into Protestant terms and so acted as an intermediary between Pugin and William Morris. Morris secularized many of Pugin's ideas and his approach to medieval art was not quite so literal as Pugin's. He was the first to organize protests against the excessive restorations carried out in his day, but more seriously he was concerned with art as a form of social protest. He hoped, indeed, for a return to medieval barbarism which would destroy the complaisant industrial civilization of his day. This desire informed his political ideas as well as his literary and artistic taste. His programme never approached reality but through his disciples Morris had a strong, if marginal, influence on the trappings of Catholic worship. The arts and crafts movement which his disciples formed never acquired any overwhelming architectural context. Nevertheless, its influence was felt on the Continent and was one of the most important ingredients which went into the making of modern architecture.

By the time the Gothic revival began to influence the architectural setting of Catholic worship, requirements had, in fact, changed a great deal. During the eighteenth century various attempts were made to reform liturgical practice and turn away from the form of devotion which has left its mark on all Baroque churches in those splendid altar pieces which centre on the throne for the exposition of the sacrament; while at the same time attempts were also made to reduce the Baroque sermon to more reasonable proportions. The various attempts, particularly in Western Germany and France, to raise congregational enthusiasm for participation in the liturgy—attempts which were motivated by a search for a pure, primitive form of Latin worship—came to grief with the Catholic reaction of the 1820's. The great effort for liturgical reform was finally initiated and consolidated by such men as Abbot Guéranger (who re-founded the monastery of Solesmes in 1833). This monastery became the centre for the reform of liturgical music based on the Gregorian chant and of educating the laity in proper liturgical practice. Guéranger was an apostle of the Primacy of Rome and of the superiority of the Roman use over all other liturgical practice. At its outset, therefore, the liturgical movement turned against episcopal independence and experiment in matters of worship to centralized discipline. Within a matter of a few years Guéranger's reforms were taken up by the High Church party in Britain, particularly by the Tractarian movement, as well as by the more sacramentally minded German Protestants.

In spite of the extreme Romanizing of the reformers the buildings did not conform to any great extent to the primitive Roman model. In France and Britain and in Germany, Gothic had been accepted as a style suitable for church building and Solesmes abbey itself was restored as a Gothic building. Even in the cases where new materials were being used for church building, as in Boileau's big iron church, St Eugène in Paris, the Gothic fancy-dress remained essential and although later buildings such as Baltard's St Augustine, also in Paris (1867), tended to draw on much more diversified architectural precedent, on the whole the Gothic style dominated church building. This is noticeable in England where many church buildings were put up in the newly developing industrial towns during the second half of the nineteenth century. The Roman Catholic community in particular expended a great deal of energy on its churches. The return of the Catholic hierarchy in 1850 created a demand for cathedral buildings and the slow return of monastic communities also had its effect. Designers such as Pugin made an impact outside the Catholic community and the English Gothic revival came to be a dominating force in world architecture. It is a tribute to its popularity that the great church of St Nicholas in Hamburg (1845–63) was built to designs by Sir Giles Gilbert Scott.

On the whole, the American situation continued to reflect the English one at one remove. One of the most impressive ecclesiastical buildings of the first half of the century, Benjamin Latrobe's Roman Catholic cathedral in Baltimore (begun in 1805) has a chilly, papery, dignified neo-classic interior and a curiously incoherent exterior. Latrobe produced alternative classic and Gothic schemes for this church. Later in the century, when American dependence on Paris-trained builders replaces the British influence, things change for the better; a most impressive church structure, in fact one of the most impressive nineteenth-century buildings in America if not in the world, is H. H. Richardson's Trinity church in Boston (1872–7). It is a huge and splendidly articulated neo-Romanesque structure; but Trinity church was conceived as a vehicle for a great preacher and in fact the bulk of church architecture in the States was conceived in this way and so, therefore, cut off from the strong liturgical stream of church building in Europe.

Various attempts were made during the latter part of the nineteenth century to get away from the Gothic dressing-up of church architecture and ornament. A concerted effort, for instance, was made by the monks of Beuron Abbey in South West Germany to found a new ecclesiastical style on independent unhistorical principles. Over and over again these attempts failed, largely because a coherent visual approach must be the product of a diversified community and cannot be artificially devised by a particular group for its own end; inevitably the devisers found that they cut themselves off from the rest of the society, and so defeated their own ends.

But on the whole church architecture followed current fashions and was imitative and eclectic by turns. Towards the end of the nineteenth century the liturgical revival sloughed off its Gothic preferences in favour of various early Christian and Romanesque themes. The Abbey of St André in Belgium became an influential centre of the Romanesque revival. By a curious coincidence the first important building in reinforced concrete, a material which was to be so important for the future of architecture, was the little church of St John at Montmartre in Paris, by Anatole de Baudot (1894–7). The St John of Montmartre made only a marginal contribution to the future development of concrete architecture; the architect who was to develop a new approach to church design was Auguste Perret, who began to build at the beginning of the century but whose first big ecclesiastical commission was the church of Our Lady at Raincy, just outside Paris in 1922–3. All his subsequent church buildings were based on the approach he developed at Raincy. The building was light and airy and a structure of thin supports carried a concrete vault. The walls were made of a concrete fretwork filled with stained glass, so that they became a continuous diaphragm of highly coloured glass, broken by the heavy pattern of concrete glazing.

The obvious medieval analogy to this kind of construction was grafted on to Perret's formal, even classical, approach; an approach very much in sympathy with that of many of the best French engineers and builders. Perret did not concern himself over much with current liturgical thinking which already in his day was tending away from the solemnity and formalism which he took for granted. On the other hand, Perret's classicism had an enormously powerful impact on many of his contemporaries. The architect who did, however, attempt to develop a theoretical approach to church building in sympathy with the liturgical movement was the German Rudolph Schwartz, who was also a very prolific builder of churches in Germany. Unlike Perret's, however, Schwartz's ideas were more specifically about church building and less about architecture in general. His buildings belong slightly outside the main

architectural tendencies of our time. Although one is grate-
ful, therefore, for his initiative in leavening the lower
reaches of church building in the German-speaking lands,
his contribution to future development is limited by his
own isolation from the main current of architectural
thinking.

Church building must operate in the forms which are
essential to the architecture of its own day. Our whole conception of architecture has been altered very radically in
the last two decades. Churches no longer tower over their
surroundings but, on the contrary, are dwarfed by tall
blocks of dwellings or offices. Increasingly buildings are
made by industrial methods. There is no longer any question of appealing to historical styles; and there is an increasing dependence on the developing style of our own
day. Even the most diehard traditionalists have, in the
last ten years, become reconciled to the state of affairs, but
this reconciliation does not mean, as yet, that ecclesiastical authority is prepared to give creative and encouraging
patronage to modern architects. The churches in which
clear thinking about the meaning of the Christian liturgy
is allied with creative architectural procedure are extremely
few. Corbusier, perhaps the greatest architect of our times,
he died in 1965, designed two churches—the pilgrimage
chapel at Ronchamp and the church of the Dominican
priory outside Lyons. A young French designer, Rainer
Senn, is acutely aware of both the liturgical and pastoral
problems confronting the builders of new churches; he has
therefore made tentative approaches towards reshaping the
church entirely in a spirit of great seriousness and with
admirable economy of means.

Senn and Corbusier are not alone in being aware of the
seriousness of the situation. Several other attempts have
been made to translate the essentials of church planning
into the formal terms of modern architecture: as, for instance, at St John's Abbey, Collegeville, Minnesota, by
Marcel Breuer, or at Our Lady of the Poor in Milan by

Gino Figini and Luigi Pollini. Several other buildings have
been designed by Marcel Breuer: among them Annuncia-
tion convent and academy at Bismarck, North Dakota, and
the more recent church of St Francis de Sales in Muskegon,
Michigan. Unfortunately Marcel Breuer's ecclesiastical
work has shown a very considerable falling off. In general
it might be said that in comparison with Jewish and Protestant church buildings Catholic U.S.A. has done con-
spicuously badly. Individual achievements in South
American cities, the church of St Francis at Pampulha in
Brazil, by Niemeyer, and the two churches at Puerto Ordaz
by Batallia Quinand and Bena Certaf considerably exceed
any individual achievement in the U.S.A. It is to be hoped
that the next decade will witness a flowering of the talents
of an increasing number of young architects who will grow
to maturity in a creative and dynamic expression as the
opportunities present themselves.

The contrast between Senn's and Corbusier's approach
may most usefully show up the real problems which the
modern church architect still has to solve. In fact the
contrast between the two approaches is inherent in the
whole current architectural situation. Senn designs
churches of little pretension and of schematic appearance.
His early allegiance to Abbé Pierre of the Emmaus community has informed his search for a form of church
building in which methods of industrial production can be
deployed towards creating a volume in which the community participates as much as possible in the liturgical
offering. His buildings, however, never rise much above
the commonplace. The spaces are as schematic as the
elevations and no real attempt is made to see what sort of
a volume is generated by the renewed vision of the altar
and its setting in Christian worship. A church by Senn,
therefore, will never be offensively assertive in the non-
Christian environment of the twentieth-century housing
estate; inoffensive in the sense in which the great nine-

teenth-century cathedrals built in the "style" of Tunisia or of Japan were offensive to the native inhabitants of those regions. The emphasis in Senn's building is on the mass-produced, the temporary, the adaptable: their inoffensiveness, however, suggests that by avoiding risk they avoid also the possibility of making any great plastic contribution to the environment in which they are placed.

Corbusier's two churches have different virtues: they are definitely conceived as unique buildings, suitable only for the one position for which they are destined. The long, ship-like chancel of the chapel of the Dominican house at Latourette could perhaps, with slight modifications, be turned into the nave of a normal church, but the long narrow shape is, of course, inherently much more suitable to the antiphonal singing of a choir of religious than to the more amorphous worship of a parish community. In the case of the Ronchamps chapel the building is even more idiosyncratic, as it was conceived entirely in response to the extraordinary position of the pilgrimage chapel on the summit of the hill overlooking the landscape. Ronchamps, however, proposes problems of an order which is not even implied in Senn's pedestrian projects: although it is a building of a high originality, intended for a particular occasion, it is nevertheless evocative of a whole sequence of ideas associated with church buildings, many of which were discussed earlier on in the book. The closed wall, pitted with tiny windows, which faces the approaching pilgrim, suggests a fortress—the billowing form of the roof, a tent; but also, in combination with the funnel-shaped towers and the sharp edge of the corner which cuts into the hill, it carries the suggestion of a ship. The light which these tower funnels admit to the interior suggests a catacomb, while the movement implied by the naval suggestions is maintained by the axial urgency of the curved ceiling, detached from the earthbound walls by a thin strip of light. It is difficult to say how many of these associations were present in the mind of the architect at the time he was working on the building. In any case, none of these features is literally recorded in the structure and appearance of the building. They are allusions which the architect has conceived while considering the more obvious problems connected with the design of building a pilgrimage chapel: problems such as the relationship of altars for the open-air Masses to that inside the church building, of the position of the venerated statue and of the small practical problems involved in such a structure.

Corbusier's church provides an enormously rich experience for the spectator, not only by virtue of its simple but marvellously modulated volume but also because it appeals to a rich deposit of traditional associations which a more pedestrian designer will deliberately ignore. In the present situation of the arts, or rather of architecture in particular, the provision of quantity appears to be the overriding consideration with the patrons, the people who pay for the buildings, if not always with the designers. Church authorities are no exception. In any case, Corbusier was a great architect; his kind appear only once every two or three generations, and unfortunately church authorities were slow to use his services. It may well be objected that in the growing housing estates and new towns the provision of an assembly space for the church is the overriding consideration, and the matter of plastic quality in church building or the equally subjective matter of associative richness are not pastoral considerations but rather a dressing to the otherwise essential building. This view, however, smacks of over-simplification. Christianity is a religion concerned intensely with the quality of individual response and in these last years the liturgical movement has made us acutely aware of the way in which the words and gestures of the liturgy carry the Christian message into a dialogue between the officiants and the people during the Eucharist. The liturgical movement, however, has expressed itself in words and in music and all too little attention has been paid to the church building as a teaching environment. Now, clearly, Christian people no longer need to be taught in pictures as a substitute for the printed word. Illiteracy has become a marginal problem for the church builders, though it may occupy the forefront of the attention of some missionaries. Though, of course, church decoration was only in a subsidiary sense used for teaching: in the sense that the chanting of the Gospel in the liturgy is not intended as a substitute for private study of the Gospel but as a solemn reminder and reiteration of words which are already familiar to the hearers. So the elaborate sculpture frontispieces of medieval churches were not simply diagrams for teaching doctrine but were solemn memorials of theological verities given a definite context in the whole plan and structure of the church building which, in its turn, was an analogy of the Church and of the created world.

The greatness of medieval church building, indeed of all church building, is bound up with the solemn proclamation of the truths of the Christian religion in visual as well as verbal terms. This visual setting out of theological truth is not simply a fancy cultural top dressing, agreeable in times of plenty, but completely unimportant in the present time of stress; it is an essential pastoral need of the living Church.

In every circumstance of life the Church must be able to bear witness to its own true nature and to its belief about the nature of man before the secular world. In the particular circumstances of our own times it is essential that the Church should not only make expository statements about doctrine but also in its public actions maintain its faith in the quality of human experience as it is enshrined in the public worship of the Christian body, in the gestures and the music which accompany it and in the visual setting in which it takes place. The Church has always set out to take into itself and sanctify the environment of everyday life. Our contemporaries are obsessed with issues of mass housing and of quantity in building. Against this the church building must reassert the value of quality: but reassert it in terms which are neither archaic nor eccentric. Returning to the work of the two architects just mentioned, it seems that Senn is not in his work aware of the larger problems with which an architect of Corbusier's greatness is able to deal confidently. But then, we may have to wait another century before an architect of Corbusier's genius appears again. This, however, does not absolve the church architect or his patron from considering the issues at stake.

The temptation is, of course, to accept the easy solution of schematic poverty; but the virtue of poverty would lie in the physical deployment of materials and the acceptance of modern methods of production and building and not in the poverty of spirit which betrays the essential task of the church builder. From the very outset church building has continued the task which all public buildings most preferred for their builders—that of commenting on the nature of the world in which we live and of mediating between the user of the building and the disorder, the menace, of the great outside world. This must always be done in terms which also visually evaluate our environment. That is, a church must to some extent be a standard to which our visual experience can be referred and by which we can also make sense of it in terms of our faith. So there is a dialogue between the church building and the rest of the environment. The neglect of this dialogue reduces church building to the business of constructing sheds of indifferent shape and annuls, devalues, the whole past of church building with which this essay has dealt. On the other hand, an escape into archaic modes or eccentric speculations cuts church building off from the daily experience of the worshipper so that he can no longer submit his daily visual experience to the sanctifying influence of the church.

SELECT BIBLIOGRAPHY

In this series: SYNDICUS, Eduard: *Early Christian Art.*

BOUYER, Louis: *Liturgical Piety*, Notre Dame, Ind., Univ. of Notre Dame Press, 1955 (English edn, *Life and Liturgy*, London, Sheed and Ward, 1956).

BRANNER, Robert: *Gothic Architecture*, London, Prentice-Hall, and New York, Braziller, 1962.

BROWN, Frank E.: *Roman Architecture*, London, Prentice-Hall, and New York, Braziller, 1962.

CHASTEL, André: *Italian Art*, London, Faber & Faber, and New York, Yoseloff, 1963.

DALTON, O. M.: *Byzantine Art and Archeology*, London, Oxford Univ. Press, 1911, and New York, Dover, 1961.

DAVIES, J. G.: *The Origin and Development of Early Christian Church Architecture*, London, SCM Press, and Naperville, Ill., Allenson, 1952; *The Architectural Setting of Baptism*, London, Barrie & Rockliff, 1960.

HAMILTON, J. Arnott: *Byzantine Architecture and Decoration*, London, Batsford, 1933, and Westwood, N.J., Revell, 1956.

HAMMOND, Peter: *Liturgy and Architecture*, London, Barrie & Rockliff, 1960, and New York, Columbia Univ. Press, 1961.

HIRN, Yrjo: *The Sacred Shrine*, Boston, Mass., Beacon, 1957, and London, Faber, 1958.

JANSON, H. W.: *A History of Art*, London, Thames & Hudson, and New York, Abrams, 1962.

JUNGMANN, Joseph A., S.J.: *The Mass of the Roman Rite, its Origins and Development*, New York, Benziger, 1951 and 1956 (two Vols).

LOWRY, Bates: *Renaissance Architecture*, London, Prentice-Hall, and New York, Braziller, 1962.

MACDONALD, William: *Early Christian and Byzantine Architecture,* London, Prentice-Hall, and New York, Braziller, 1962.

MILLON, Henry A.: *Baroque and Rococo Architecture,* London, Prentice-Hall, and New York, Braziller, 1962.

PEVSNER, Nicolaus: *An Outline of European Architecture,* Baltimore, Md., Penguin, 1960, and Harmondsworth, Pelican, 1962.

REGAMEY, P. R.: *Religious Art in the Twentieth Century,* New York, Herder & Herder, 1963.

SAALMAN, Howard: *Medieval Architecture,* London, Prentice-Hall, and New York, Braziller, 1962.

SIMSON, Otto von: *The Gothic Cathedral: the Origins of Gothic Architecture and the Medieval Concept of Order,* London, Routledge & Kegan Paul, 1956, and New York, Pantheon, 1962.

STRZYGOWSKI, Joseph: *Origin of Christian Church Art,* Oxford, The Clarendon Press, 1923.

SWIFT, Emerson H.: *Roman Sources of Christian Art,* New York, Columbia Univ. Press, 1951.

TALBOT-RICE, D.: *The Beginnings of Christian Art,* London, Hodder & Stoughton, 1957, and Nashville, Tenn., 1958.

WEBB, Geoffrey: *Architecture in Britain: the Middle Ages,* Harmondsworth, Penguin, and Baltimore, Md., Penguin, 1956.

WITTKOWER, Rudolf: *Architectural Principles in the Age of Humanism,* London, Tiranti, 1949.